IELTS TEST MASTERY

INTENSIVE ACADEMIC IELTS WORKBOOK

Stephen Slater & Simone Braverman

www.IELTS-Blog.com   www.IELTSonTrack.com

Copyright © Slater, Braverman 2024
First published 2025

Information on this title: ielts-blog.com, ieltsontrack.com

Unless otherwise indicated, all materials on these pages are copyrighted by the authors. All rights reserved. No part of this book (including text, images, audio or video content) may be used for any purpose other than non-commercial personal study use. Therefore, unauthorised reproduction, photocopying, recording, modification, storage in a retrieval system or retransmission, in any form or by any means, electronic, mechanical or otherwise, is strictly prohibited without prior written permission from the authors. Users are not permitted to mount this file on any network servers.

A catalogue record for this book is available from the National Library of Australia

ISBN: 978-0648868217

Audio: Stephen Slater

Cover design: Stephen Slater, Simone Braverman, 100Covers.com

Acknowledgements

The authors hereby acknowledge the following for their contributions to this book:

Neville Clark at Disk-Edits Pty Ltd. for audio recording and mastering.

Donna Millen for permission to use recorded extracts from IELTS on Track Listening tests.

Sally Collyns, Tanya Dahlenburg, Dr Ashish Davda, Sarah Divine, Georgina Hafteh, Peter Hanna and Keith Smith, for voice recordings.

IELTS-Blog.com members, but particularly Dharmen, Diana, Eveline, Hemanth, Hon, Irina, Juliana, Lili, Nga, Paramjit, Princess, Rae, Raza, Rodney, Shahin, Shyam, Simone, Tina, Venkatesh, Viet for participation in the trialling of the Listening and Reading test material.

Alex Braverman for assistance with proofreading and graphic design.

100covers.com for assistance in creating the cover of this book.

Freepic.com for some of the images used in this book.

Australian Geographic for permission to use the article "To dam or not to dam", originally published online at http://www.australiangeographic.com.au/journal/ on 21 January 2011.

Other texts were freshly written to test parameters drawing on and integrating information from a wide variety of written sources.

While every effort has been made to contact copyright holders it has not been possible to identify all sources of the material used. The authors and publisher would in such instances welcome information from copyright holders to rectify any errors or omissions.

Introduction

A big **'HELLO'** to you from your team of authors, Stephen and Simone. We are glad you have chosen **IELTS Test Mastery** for your exam preparation. Of course, the reason you're using this book is that you need a high IELTS score and you want to be confident about how to achieve this, either for yourself or, if you are a teacher, for your students.

IELTS Test Mastery has 3 main components:

- Full IELTS tests for you to practise under test conditions
- Full IELTS test practice activities across all the many IELTS question types
- IELTS test-taking strategies, and insights into common problems experienced by test takers

IELTS Test Mastery will encourage and help you systematically to review your individual performance on our tests so that you become more aware of yourself as an IELTS test taker, and have a better sense of your unique strengths and weaknesses under IELTS test conditions.

The most popular IELTS books often provide just one practice test after another. Naturally, many test takers believe that a full taste of test reality is all they need. **Mastery of IELTS**, however, **sees a greater need - the need for deeper understanding** of how the test functions, of its many task types, and of how you, uniquely, interact with IELTS test material, and manage your own performance. Repeating tests, and evaluating test performance is an important part of how we think test takers build this deeper understanding. **As this mastery of the test grows, the feeling of confidence and empowerment develops**, leading to a top IELTS score.

IELTS Test Mastery also offers you supplementary materials in an online, downloadable resource. In our **Treasure Chest** you will find blank answer sheets, audio recordings, sample answers to the tests and test activities and solutions to the many problems you might have when taking the IELTS test.

We are confident that **by using IELTS Test Mastery systematically**, and thereby becoming your own best teacher and manager, **you will gain the vital skills, awareness and insight needed to** reduce your nerves and **enhance your performance on IELTS Test Day**.

IELTS LISTENING

Listening Entry Test	4
Listening Test Practice	16
Listening Checkpoint Test	32

IELTS READING

Reading Entry Test	42
Reading Test Practice	58
Reading Checkpoint Test	82

IELTS WRITING

Writing Entry Test	96
Writing Task 1 Practice	102
Writing Task 2 Practice	130
Writing Checkpoint Test	162

IELTS SPEAKING

Speaking Entry Test	166
Speaking Test Practice	170
Speaking Checkpoint Test	196

COMPLETE IELTS EXIT TEST

How to Take the Exit Test	202
Complete IELTS Exit Test	204

ANSWERS

Listening Answers	228
Reading Answers	230
Writing Answers	234
Speaking Answers	242

LISTENING ENTRY TEST

IELTS Listening Section

Get Ready

This entry Listening Test is just like an actual test and will take 40 minutes - 30 minutes to listen to a recording and answer questions, and then 10 minutes to transfer answers from the question booklet to the Answer sheet.

The recording consists of four parts, which progress in speed and difficulty. Parts 1 and 3 are recordings of conversations between two or more people, and Parts 2 and 4 involve individual speakers. The format and contents of the Listening test are the same for Academic and General Training tests.

Every part will have a different topic.

Part 1 is an everyday conversation between two people, such as a patient and a doctor, a receptionist and a client, for example.

Part 2 is a lecture, a presentation or a speech by a person on an everyday topic such as services or facilities.

Part 3 is a conversation that may include more than two people about study-related matters. Often the participants are a student and a lecturer or a group of students.

Part 4 is a talk or a lecture on an academic subject - a study the speaker has undertaken, for example.

There are 40 questions in total in the Listening test, 10 questions in each part. All the questions will be about the information on the recording; however, the way you need to provide your answers, or the 'question type', will vary.

At the start of each Listening, part you will have about 15 - 20 seconds to read its group of questions before listening. Once the recording starts you must answer the questions as you listen, because **you only hear the recording once.**

How to write your answers in the IELTS Test

You won't need to rephrase any words that you hear in your answers, or change their form, just use words you hear on the recording.

You can write in uppercase or lowercase letters (e.g. 'AFTERNOON' or 'afternoon') when answering any question with missing words (such as sentence completion, summary completion, note completion, table completion, etc), but be consistent.

Correct spelling is very important. Misspelled answers may be penalized, but both British and American spelling are accepted. For example, you can write 'color' (American) or 'colour' (British), but 'calor' would be an incorrect answer and receive zero points.

Grammar is important in the Listening test! Grammatically incorrect answers will not get any points, even if their meaning is correct. If you use a singular form ('apple') where a plural ('apples') is required, or if your answer uses the wrong tense or verb form ('he go' instead of 'he goes'), you will receive zero points.

Don't use short forms in your final answers! It is OK to use shorthand writing for your notes in the question booklet on the Paper Test, but your final answers on the answer sheet must be complete. So, if you scribbled something like 'doc. ord.' in your notes, use the full form 'doctor's orders' when transferring answers to the answer sheet.

 Scan the QR code to access the **Listening Entry Test recording** *and a blank answer sheet in the Treasure Chest or visit https://ielts-blog.com/treasure-chest*

Are you ready? Start the Entry Test now.

IELTS LISTENING ENTRY TEST

Test Instructions

 Listen to the recording straight through, **ONCE** only (total audio time: 30 min). Answer the questions while listening to each section. At the end of the test, you will have another ten minutes to transfer your answers to the Answer sheet.

PART 1   **Questions 1 – 10**

Questions 1 – 6

Complete the notes below. Write **NO MORE THAN ONE WORD AND/OR A NUMBER** from the listening for each answer.

Buying a Used Car: Contact Details	
Model	Celica
Year	1985
Number of Owners	(1) _____
Condition	overall good
(2) _____	done last year
Reason for Selling:	owner going overseas to (3) _____
Asking Price:	$ (4) _____
Address:	(5) _____, Princes' St, Parkwood
Contact name:	Elena
Car Colour:	(6) _____

Questions 7 – 10

Complete the notes below. Write **NO MORE THAN ONE WORD AND/OR A NUMBER** from the listening for each answer.

Sam's car broke down and he is getting to the university by (7) _____ .

Jan needs a car because she works late in the (8) _____ and fears for her safety at night.

Sam recommends having a (9) _____ look at the car.

Sam is planning to (10) _____ his roommate's motorcycle to take Jan to Parkwood.

IELTS Listening Section

PART 2   Questions 11 – 20

Label the locations on the map below.

Write the correct letter, **A – D**, next to Questions **11 – 13**.

Questions 11 – 13

11   Grey whales often seen in this area   _____

12   Wildlife can be seen here   _____

13   The tour will stop here for 1 hour   _____

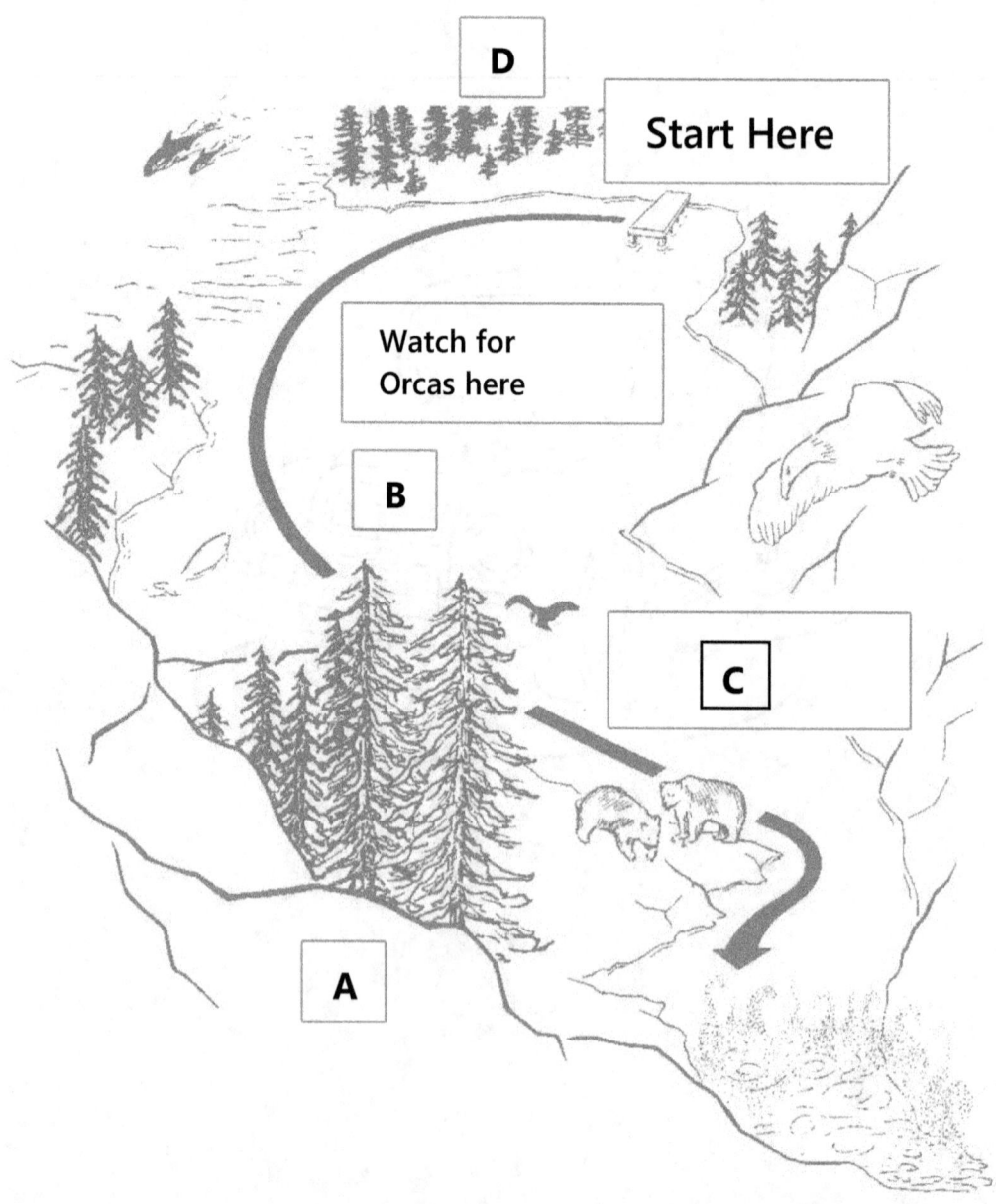

8

Questions 14 – 17

*Choose the correct letter **A**, **B** or **C**.*

14 Dolphins usually

    A   keep away from boats

    B   race killer whales

    C   swim beside the boat

15 What colour are killer whales?

    A   grey

    B   black and white

    C   blue

16 Orcas feed on

    A   seabirds

    B   shrimp

    C   grey whales

17 What size are grey whales?

    A   1-2 metres

    B   7-8 metres

    C   14 metres

IELTS Listening Section

Questions 18 – 20

*Choose the correct letter **A, B or C**.*

18 For a smooth ride, sit

    A away from the engine

    B in the middle of the boat

    C in the back of the boat

19 Survival suits

    A Are bright yellow in colour

    B Keep you warm in the water

    C Help you swim

20 Sea-sickness patches

    A Make you drowsy

    B Don't work as well as pills

    C Are to be worn on your arm

PART 3 Questions 21 – 30

Questions 21 – 23

*Choose **THREE** letters (A – E), and write them in any order in boxes **21 – 23** on your answer sheet.*

*What are the **THREE** requirements to be selected for 'Travel Documentary'?*

A   Be selected for an interview
B   Have travelled the world for 3 months
C   Complete a 4-week training course
D   Produce 5 travel documentaries from different parts of the world
E   Travel around the world and film

Questions 24 – 25

*Choose **TWO** letters (A – E), and write them in any order in boxes **24 – 25** on your answer sheet.*

*What are the **TWO** requirements of competitors for 'Travel Documentary'?*

A   Produce a 10-minute video every 2 weeks
B   Previous work experience in film-making
C   Choose 3 countries to travel to from a list prepared by competition organisers
D   Complete a course in professional photography
E   Obtain approval for travel plans

IELTS Listening Section

Questions 26 – 28

*Choose the correct letter **A, B or C**.*

26   One of the challenges competitors face is

   A   Cultural differences
   B   Communicating in a foreign language
   C   Obtaining permits to film

27   What was Sarah Price's worst experience during the trip?

   A   She got lost in Mongolia.
   B   She was homesick.
   C   She got sick in a remote place.

28   In which of the following areas does Ray expect to have most difficulty?

   A   loneliness
   B   time pressure
   C   organisation skills

Questions 29 – 30

*Choose **TWO** letters (A – E), and write them in any order in boxes **29 – 30** on your answer sheet.*

*What **TWO** things are provided free of charge to the competitors?*

   A   Flights
   B   Video editing software
   C   Accommodation
   D   Restaurant meals
   E   Local tour guide

PART 4   Questions 31 – 40

Questions 31 – 40

*Complete the notes below. Write **NO MORE THAN ONE WORD AND/OR A NUMBER** from the listening for each answer.*

The letters QWERTY are located in the (**31**) _____ row of the keyboard. This arrangement originated to solve a problem with early (**32**) _____. Contrary to popular belief, QWERTY layout wasn't designed to slow typists but did result in (**33**) _____ for them. In 1932 August Dvorak solved the inefficiency problem by re-designing the (**34**) _____ of the typewriter. He put the most commonly used letters on the home row. Using the Dvorak keyboard, (**35**) _____ % of all work can be done from the home row. In contrast, only (**36**) _____ words can be typed from the home row on the QWERTY keyboard. Other advantages of the Dvorak keyboard include a 50% improvement in (**37**) _____ in typing and a 15 – 20% increase in (**38**) _____. But the most important difference is in finger movement. Typists using the QWERTY keyboard moved their fingers up to (**39**) _____ miles per day compared to one mile a day for Dvorak typists. The main reason why Dvorak system wasn't adopted was (**40**) _____.

The answers are located in the IELTS Answers section at the end of this book.

Score, Review then Practise

Score your Entry Test

Now you have finished the Entry Test, check the answers, located in the IELTS Answers section at the end of this book.

Add up your total score out of 40. Remember that your spelling has to be correct, and your answers must be in the correct place.

Review

Once you know your total score, go back to your answers and try to identify the kinds of errors you made, and the way you proceeded through the test and questions.

- Were your errors mainly in the later sections?
- What question types did you find the most difficult?
- Did you hear some information incorrectly?
- Were the voices too fast?
- Were your spellings and grammar accurate?

Use questions like those above to build a personal profile of your performance.

Practise

Once your review is complete, move on to the next section of this book and practise all the question types used in IELTS Listening, especially the types that are still difficult for you.

Boost Your Performance

For any listening activities that you still find troublesome, check the useful test strategies given (Page 25) and ways to solve common test-taking problems (Page 30). Then try those challenging listening activities again, and change any of your answers that seem wrong.

LISTENING TEST PRACTICE

WHAT'S INSIDE:

- Practise the Question Types
- Boost Your Performance

IELTS Listening Section

Practise the Question Types

QUESTION TYPE 1   Matching Information

Tasks that involve matching information provide a group of questions and a group of answer options. The questions will be in the same order as on the recording, but the answer options will not.

It is important to focus on questions, not answer options, because the questions allow you to follow the recording, whereas answer options are presented in a random order.

Complete this listening activity to practise an example of matching information questions

In this activity you match the name of the student with the information that they give about themselves. **The best strategy** is to read the information in the questions first, before listening, so that you know what to listen out for. This is a good strategy which gives a real focus to your listening.

Activity 1   *Scan the QR code to access the **recordings for Activities 1-11** in the Treasure Chest or visit https://ielts-blog.com/treasure-chest*

 Listen to three students Anna (**A**), Veronica (**V**) and Chris (**C**) introducing themselves. Match each student with their personal information, by writing either **A, V or C**.

1 _____ is Swedish.

2 _____ was a member of a university film society.

3 _____ is studying English literature.

4 _____ wrote for a student publication.

5 _____ has already been in the festival organising committee.

6 _____ will recommend some changes in a written report.

A	Anna
V	Veronica
C	Chris

The answers are located in the IELTS Answers section at the end of this book.

QUESTION TYPE 2   Multiple Choice

With Multiple choice questions, not all answer options have the same chances of being correct. Of the three answer options (A, B, C) one is usually plain wrong or is not mentioned by the speaker, leaving you with just two options to choose from, and making your job much easier.

The best strategy before listening is to look through each set of A,B,C choices and cross out any that look (from common sense or knowledge!) unlikely to be correct. This saves time and gives the task more focus when actually listening.

Later, you might cross out an answer when a speaker says something which is **opposite** to one or other of the answer choices.

It doesn't always work, but see if you can cross out unlikely answers now, before listening to the next extract.

Complete this listening activity

Activity 2

 Listen to this short extract on food trends. Choose **A**, **B** or **C**.

1. Mobile meals are:
   A   a form of junk food
   B   Canadian home cooking
   C   foods consumed outside of the home

2. The increase in sales of snack foods in three years could be:
   A   14%
   B   40%
   C   4%

3. Which of these is a nutritious, portable food?
   A   Muesli bar
   B   Cholesterol bar
   C   Food bar

QUESTION TYPE 3   Sentence Completion

This type of question involves writing the appropriate word in terms of meaning in the correct grammatical form. **The best strategy** is to:

- Read the task instructions to see what the maximum number of words is for each answer.
- Look through each sentence before listening and decide what type of word is required grammatically (e.g. noun? adjective? verb? adverb?).
- When you listen, choose your word and make sure it is spelled correctly.

Complete this listening activity

Activity 3

Complete these sentences using **ONE WORD ONLY** from the recording.

1   Money for the film festival comes from advertising and charging for _____.

2   It is necessary to _____ the films by the beginning of March.

3   The deadline for getting sponsors is the _____ of March.

4   The end of March is the deadline for program _____.

5   During April, posters need to be put together and _____.

QUESTION TYPE 4   Short-answer Questions

This type of question is a straightforward Q/A style. You are simply listening for the information that actually answers the question.

The best strategy is to read the questions so that you know what type of answers you are listening out for and in what order. Remember the maximum number of words you can use for each answer.

Complete this listening activity

Activity 4

 Write an answer to each question using **NO MORE THAN TWO WORDS OR NUMBERS** from the recording.

1   What did the invention of the QWERTY typewriter keyboard reduce? _____

2   What negative outcome for typists did the layout of the QWERTY keyboard cause? _____

3   On which side are many of the most frequently used typewriter keys? _____

4   What happened to typewriter technology after the QWERTY keyboard was invented? _____

IELTS Listening Section

QUESTION TYPE 5   Form Completion

This question type tests your 'orientational awareness', for example where to look on the form, and which part of the form to focus on while listening. So, **the best strategy** is to look at any form carefully before listening so that you know your way around it.

- Often the speaker will make a little mistake with an address or number and then correct it, so listen out for this type of little trick.
- When a speaker reads out a name for you to copy down and spells it out, you need to know how each of the alphabet letters is pronounced in English.
- Don't forget to check the task instructions for the maximum number of words/numbers you can use.

Complete these listening activities

Activity 5

 Listen to the airline passenger and complete the form, using **NO MORE THAN THREE WORDS OR NUMBERS**.

Passenger Enquiry Form

Arrival Flight No.   **1** _____   Time of arrival: **2** _____

Item lost: **3** _____   Country of flight connection: **4** _____

Activity 6

 Listen and complete the address and phone number.

Name: Jenny Lee

Address: **1** _____ , Riverside

Phone: **2** _____

Activity 7

 Listen and complete the information about the ATS Office, using **ONE WORD OR A NUMBER**.

ATS Office Regency Theatre

Opening times: Monday – **1** _____ 10 – 5pm,
Friday/Saturday 10 – **2** _____ pm.

Website address: **3** www._____.com

QUESTION TYPE 6   Table Completion

Again, this type of question requires you to 'know your way around' the table before listening.

The best strategy is to check the headings at the top of each column, and to check the information that is already there so that you can see what type of information is required. Oh, and don't forget to **check the task instructions for the maximum number of words**.

Complete this listening activity

Activity 8

 Listen and complete the table using **ONE WORD ONLY** for each answer.

Student Name	Work Experience Location	Day / Time of Day
Theresa	Uni **1** _____	Friday **2** _____
Manuel	Mainly **3** _____	Friday afternoons
Henry	The **4** _____ Shop	**5** _____ afternoons

IELTS Listening Section

QUESTION TYPE 7 — Summary completion

When completing a summary, it is often hard to guess straightaway which word is missing from the blank space. Sometimes it may seem as though no word is missing at all! **The best strategy** is to look at the words immediately before and after the gap, because they reveal whether the missing word is a noun, an adjective, or a verb.

For instance, consider the summary below:

> Peter and Mary are planning a **14** _____ together. The **15** _____ they have decided to visit include Canada and USA, where they will be **16** _____ by plane.
>
> It seems that answer 14 should be a noun (such as 'trip'), 15 – also a noun (such as 'countries'), and 16 should be a verb (such as 'arriving' or 'travelling').

How does this help? Once you know that you're looking for a verb, selecting the right one from what you hear on the recording will be easier. You will pay more attention to verbs than to nouns or adjectives.

In this question type, sometimes you are given a list of words to choose from for the spaces, sometimes not. If no word list is given use words that you actually hear on the recording.

Other good strategies:

- Read the summary and decide what kind of word is missing grammatically.
- Decide too, what sort of meaning the missing word might have (e.g. is it a positive, negative word, a description, a fact?)
- Check the task instructions for the maximum number of words.

Summary completion is difficult so it is often used in the later parts of the IELTS Listening test.

Complete this listening activity

Activity 9

Listen to this short talk about the Dvorak typewriter keyboard and complete the summary. Use **ONE WORD ONLY** from the talk for each space.

Although the Dvorak keyboard is superior it has not been **1** _____ for two main reasons: the Depression, and **2** _____ . Too many people were too accustomed to the QWERTY keyboard. This has prevented improved keyboard **3** _____ for 70+ years.

IELTS Listening Section

| QUESTION TYPE 8 | Diagram Labeling |

This type of question is similar to forms and tables in the sense that you need to 'know your way around' the diagram BEFORE listening, in order to be more relaxed when listening.

The best strategy is to look at all the information given and what any labels refer to, then you know more about the topic and about the type of information to listen out for. As usual, check the maximum number of words/numbers in the task instructions.

Complete this listening activity

Activity 10

 Listen and complete the notes in the diagrams. Use **NO MORE THAN TWO WORDS** from the recording for each answer.

Before your talk

Make **2** _____ on small cards

Choose your topic and decide **1** _____ you will talk for

During your talk

3 _____ is vital when talking to an audience

Practise **4** _____ to help pronunciation

IELTS Test Mastery :: Academic

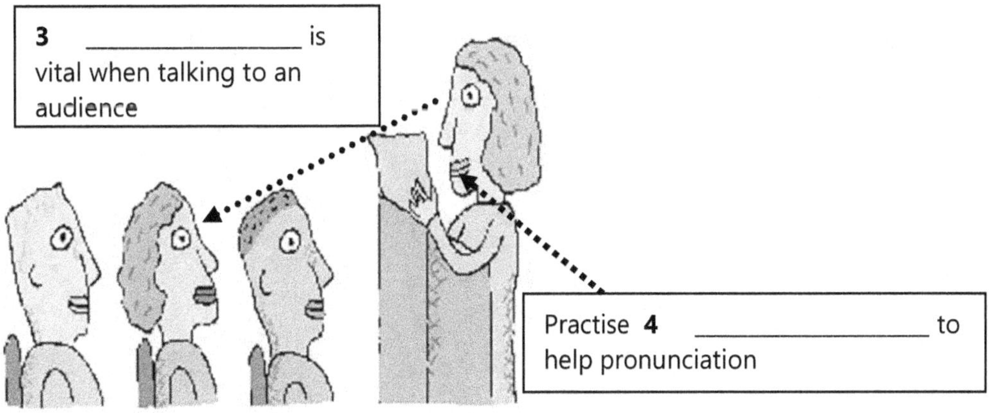

IELTS Listening Section

QUESTION TYPE 9   Map Labeling

As soon as the recording begins talking about the map/plan/diagram, **the best strategy** is to start labeling the locations on the drawing in the question booklet. Note every location the recording mentions, not just the locations required in the questions. Why? Because it is easier to write down information as the recording proceeds than it is to analyse that input at the same time. Later on, during the time given to check your answers to that particular Listening part, look at your notes and use them to find the right answers and write them in the booklet. At the end of the Listening test you will be given time to copy the correct answers on to the Answer Sheet.

Complete this listening activity

Activity 11

 Listen and label the map below.

    A   Post Office
    B   Bank
    C   Primary School
    D   Petrol Station
    E   Kindergarten

Boost Your Performance

Work through the following strategies and solutions, keeping in mind any of the listening activities that proved difficult for you.

Try the listening activities you found difficult again, changing any answers that seem wrong. Check your answers and keep practising any question types that you still find troublesome.

Strategies for Answering Problem Questions

1. Write an answer as soon as you hear it

Listening tests move through time relentlessly so you need to keep up. The continuous flow of information from the recorded voices will overrun your memory's ability to store answers, so as soon as you hear an answer to a question, write it down.

Writing may distract you from listening, at first, but with practice, you will learn to write and listen at the same time.

2. Only look at one group of questions at a time

The Listening test recordings are divided into Parts 1 to 4, but Parts 1 to 3 are divided into smaller subparts, making your job a bit easier.

In Parts 1 to 3 the spoken instructions will refer to a smaller group of questions within the part, *not all the questions*, and the voice will tell you which question group to look at. For example, in Part 1 (covering questions 1-10) the voice may say, 'Now look at questions 7-10' (followed by 20 seconds of silence). This means that in the listening test portion after that, you only need to answer questions 7, 8, 9 and 10.

Best strategies? Most importantly, **read the questions** while the recording is silent, but don't read beyond the final one in the group (Question 10 in our example). **Underline key words**, quickly **grasp the main idea** of each question and **imagine the sort of answer you will hear**— an amount? working hours? a location?

Listening parts 1–3 are broken down into subparts so you won't lose a whole part even if you've missed a couple of answers. So, for example, if you hear the recording say "Now look at questions 11 to 13", but you still don't have the answer to question 10, immediately stop looking for that answer and move on to questions 11-13. This gives you a chance to answer all the questions in that new group and not get left behind. Then, at the end, go back and guess the answer to 'lost' question 10.

3. Pay attention to detail

Any specific information on a recording, such as names, phone numbers, dates, opening hours, locations, years, colours is usually mentioned for a reason. Such details may well be contained in the answer. When you hear specific information on a recording, look again at the current group of questions, to see where it may fit.

4. Do not let the use of synonyms confuse you

It may happen that you will hear a word on the recording, but the question will instead use its synonym. Test takers whose minds are 'locked' on the exact word the speaker said, may get confused and not realize the question is mentioning the same thing.

> **Example**
>
> The recording may say,
> "The list of prohibited items inside an airplane includes..."
>
> but the question may say,
> "Passengers are not allowed to take the following items on board a plane".

5. Expect the speakers to change their minds

One of the things you are being tested on in the Listening test is your ability to follow the *development of the conversation*. Just like in a real-life conversation, speakers on a recording can change their minds. Pay attention to such developments in the conversation, don't be tricked into a wrong answer.

> **Example**
>
> Peter: "We can book a flight on the 10th of April, what do you think?"
>
> Mary: "My vacation request was approved to start from the 9th, so I am free to go. But hang on, isn't your brother's birthday party on the 10th?"
>
> Peter: "You're right, how could I forget?! Thanks for reminding me. We'd better book our flight on the 11th of April, or he'll never forgive me."

Avoid these common mistakes

Many correct answers get disqualified for 'technical' reasons. To make sure this doesn't happen to you, read through these common problems to avoid making mistakes.

Mistake 1: **Not following the task instructions.**

Every task type has a clear set of instructions specifying how many words or numbers you can use, and what you need to do—complete a sentence, answer a question, circle a letter, and so on. Do *exactly* as the instructions say. If the instructions say "Circle two letters", do exactly that—don't circle just one or three letters.

Especially important is the word limit. Answers that consist of more words than the limit allows, will get no points even if the meaning is correct. If the instructions say, **"WRITE NO MORE THAN THREE WORDS"**, you may write one, or two or three words—but never more than three.

Mistake 2: **Transferring or entering information incorrectly.**

Words

In the Paper Test, only the missing words should be written on the answer sheet when transferring answers from the question booklet (for the Computer Test version, these are typed in the gap).

For instance, consider a task that asks you to complete a sentence using **NO MORE THAN THREE WORDS AND/OR A NUMBER**.

Example

The sentence is: "Peter and Mary **are** * _____ **to** visit their relatives in Ottawa"

Since the correct answer is 'not going', writing the words 'are not going to' on the answer sheet will mean receiving zero points for your answer.

Note: the definite and indefinite articles 'the', 'a' count as one word each.

IELTS Listening Section

Mistake 3: Entering unnecessary symbols and abbreviations

If you are required to complete a sentence that talks about money such as,

"The deposit Peter has to pay for plane tickets is **$**_____"

write *only the amount* on the answer sheet, without the '$' sign, because it's already written in the question booklet.

In a sentence that talks about time, such as,

"Trading hours of the travel agency are Mon–Fri, _____ **am** to 5 pm."

write only the time on the answer sheet, without the 'am'. The reason is that 'am' is already written in the booklet and you do not need to repeat it.

Mistake 4: Confusing numbers with digits

Confusing numbers with digits is a common problem. The word 'digit' means any of 0, 1, 2, 3, 4, 5, 6, 7, 8, and 9. A number is a combination of digits, so a number may have more than one digit.

Why is this important? Because when instructions ask to 'answer in **NO MORE THAN THREE WORDS AND/OR A NUMBER**', it is a mistake to think that you are only allowed to write one digit in the space provided on the answer sheet. You are allowed to write one number, which can consist of many digits.

Example

Complete the sentence below using **NO MORE THAN THREE WORDS AND/OR A NUMBER.**

"The address of Peter's uncle is *_____ Main street, Moncton, New Brunswick, Canada."

*Let's say the correct answer (the missing house number) is '308'. It's a mistake to think that you're allowed only to write a single digit (such as '3'), in fact you are allowed to, and should, write '308'.

Mistake 5: Transferring full answers instead of their letters

When the task instructions ask you to choose a letter, this is exactly what you need to transfer to the answer sheet—the letter, not the full answer. This only applies to IELTS On Paper, because in IELTS On Computer you click on the answer to select it and you don't transfer the answer to the answer sheet.

There is a whole set of reasons why you shouldn't copy the full answer:

1. It's not what the instructions say
2. You can make a spelling mistake
3. It takes longer to write two or three words than to write a letter.

> **Example**
>
> Choose the correct letter **A – C**.
>
> The reason Mary prefers to stay in this hotel is
> A   because of the magnificent view
> B*   because of the facilities
> C   because of the affordable pricing
>
> *Let's say B is the correct answer. While you are listening, circle B in the question booklet. When transferring the answers to the answer sheet, write 'B' in the relevant space—don't copy the words 'because of the facilities'.

IELTS Listening Section

Solving Problems During the Listening Test

In preparation for the Listening test you may have trouble with some aspects of the test and you're not sure what to do. Don't worry! This is a normal part of the process. By dealing with these issues in the early stages of your preparation you will make sure they don't affect you in the real test! Here are some of the most common problems, and solutions to them.

Problem 1: I can't understand what is being said on the recording

Problem 2: I lose track of the recording

Problem 3: I don't have enough time to read the questions before the recording begins playing

Problem 4: I am not good at spelling

Problem 5: I am unsure what the correct answer is

Problem 6: I have a hearing/eyesight problem

Problem 7: I don't feel well on the day of my exam

 *Scan the QR code to download the **solutions for these problems** from the Treasure Chest or visit https://ielts-blog.com/treasure-chest*

LISTENING CHECKPOINT TEST

IELTS Listening Section

Get Ready for the Checkpoint Test

You now have a better idea of yourself as a Listening test performer, of what types of task you will face in the IELTS test, plus some helpful strategies to boost your score.

Feeling confident?

If you feel confident, move straight on to the IELTS Listening Checkpoint test on the next page. Before you start, think about your profile - your strengths and weaknesses when taking this type of test.

 *Scan the QR code to access the **Listening Checkpoint Test** recording and a blank answer sheet in the Treasure Chest or visit https://ielts-blog.com/treasure-chest*

Feeling less confident?

If you are still struggling to master all the many aspects of the IELTS Listening test, your best strategy is to go back and repeat the Entry test again.

Doing the Entry test again has several advantages:

- You will recognise the voices, topics and content and can focus on your answers more easily

- You will be more relaxed and will understand better how not to panic

- You will remember some of your previous answers and know how to correct them and why they were wrong.

After repeating the entry test, score yourself again. Was your score higher? Even if it is, review your weaknesses again, and then move on to the Checkpoint test.

IELTS LISTENING CHECKPOINT TEST

Test Instructions

 Listen to the recording straight through, **ONCE** only (total audio time: 30 min). Answer the questions while listening to each section. At the end of the test, you will have another ten minutes to transfer your answers to the Answer sheet.

PART 1   Questions 1 – 10

Questions 1 – 5

Complete the Seafront Backpacker hostel enquiry notes.

Write **ONE WORD AND/OR A NUMBER** for each answer.

Hostel Enquiry Notes

Guest's Current Address : (1) _____ The Esplanade, Dune Beach

Guest Name :   Jacqui Wong

Mobile no. : 014 803 997   (2) _____ (correct mobile no.)

Total no. of beds available: 8 in Dormitory A, (3) _____ in Dormitory B

Cost per night Dormitory B: (4) $ _____ (weekly $90)

One-week vacancy available: Yes (other guest cancelled as (5) _____ is unwell)

IELTS Listening Section

Questions 6 – 10

*Choose the correct letter **A**, **B** or **C**.*

Write the correct letter in the boxes 6-10 on your answer sheet.

6   Which two facilities at the hostel do you need to pay for?

         A   parking and bikes

         B   towels and internet

         C   parking and towels

7   The receptionist suggests cyclists should use the road off the Esplanade mainly because

         A   it's near to the hotel on the Esplanade

         B   it's safer

         C   it's quiet and narrow

8   Bicycles can be kept

         A   in a safe

         B   in the hostel store

         C   in the garage

9   The manager owns a pet

         A   fox

         B   dog

         C   cat

10   The guest's problem with cat fur causes her to

         A   develop red skin

         B   feel rash

         C   rush outside

PART 2   Questions 11 – 20

Complete the table below.

Write **ONE WORD ONLY** for each answer.

Name of machine	Positive (+) features	Negative (–) features	Overall Assessment
Coffee Supreme	can brew 4+ cups of (11) _____ or strong coffee water filtration improves taste overflow (12) _____ and drip stop easy replacement of parts	no (13) _____ coffee grinder only 750 watt	good (14) _____ but limited performance
Café Delight	coffee maker and espresso machine (15) _____ nozzle + frothing attachment	too big - 40 cm (16) _____ and 30cm high	(17) _____ and convenient
Coffeetime Automatic	can make different drinks uses an (18) _____ 'disc' to measure water volume automatically automatic cleaning / descaling	too large for some (19) _____	(20) _____ but technology used well

IELTS Listening Section

PART 3   **Questions 21 – 30**

Question 21

Choose **TWO** letters from **A – E**.

21   Which are purposes of the Student Support Service?

    A   to aid student dependence

    B   to aid awareness of the two different cultures

    C   to study with the students

    D   to assist with developing human bonds

    E   to help students make judgements

Questions 22 – 26

Complete the report below.

Write **ONE WORD ONLY** for each answer.

STUDY PROBLEMS REPORT - Wilson

Wilson has problems with writing, not with lectures or (**22**) _____.

He can't seem to understand titles, especially key (**23**) _____ or inference.

Not good at finding enough readings or making a satisfactory (**24**) _____.

His essays are often (**25**) _____ and poorly structured.

Recommendation

Make appointment with tutor to talk about his essay (**26**) _____ at Tuesday sessions.

Questions 27 – 30

Answer the questions below.

Write **NO MORE THAN TWO WORDS** for each answer.

27   What does Grace consider a waste of time? _____

28   How would Grace feel about talking to a lecturer? _____

29   Grace is worried about her course, her sick grandmother and what else? _____

30   With whom could Grace discuss her personal issues at greater length? _____

IELTS Listening Section

PART 4 **Questions 31 – 40**

Questions 31 – 35

Write **ONE WORD ONLY** for each answer

Researchers now realise that (**31**) _____ have a major effect on positive relationships in the workplace.

Emotional intelligence fundamentally concerns a set of (**32**) _____ linked to each individual's emotions.

(**33**) _____ is basically the ability to put yourself in another person's shoes, emotionally.

Managing your emotions positively, can assist you to (**34**) _____ your whole being.

Being good with people is the key hallmark of an (**35**) _____ leader.

Questions 36 - 40

Choose the correct letter **A, B** or **C**.

According to what the lecturer says:

36 A happy workplace is a place where workers

    A   trust themselves
    B   are competent technically
    C   show mutual respect

37 A positive self-image leads to

    A   a greater ability to help others
    B   positive feelings about the organisation
    C   enjoying other people's support

38 'Perceived' self suggests

    A   high self esteem
    B   a sense of your inner self
    C   knowing what others feel

39 'Desired' self involves

    A   wanting to be assertive
    B   an excessive desire to change
    C   a wish for self-improvement

40 'Presented' self involves

    A   appearing on stage
    B   doing what others expect
    C   controlling others

The answers are located in the IELTS Answers section at the end of this book.

Finished the Checkpoint test?

When you have added up your score on the Checkpoint test, repeat the review process to develop further awareness of your ongoing weaknesses, and to chart where your test techniques and understanding have improved. Repeat the checkpoint test a few days later.

At the end of this book there will be a final test for you to try (**Exit test**) but this time you should take all four parts of the IELTS test at the same sitting (Listening, Reading, Writing and Speaking), and then award scores for all parts of the Exit test.

Now, it's time to move on to the Reading section on the next page.

READING ENTRY TEST

IELTS Reading Section

Get Ready

In the IELTS Reading test you will be asked to read three passages and answer questions on each passage. There are **3 long texts** (up to 2750 words in total) and **40 questions**. The Reading test takes **60 minutes**. During this time, you should finish reading the texts and answering the questions.

You need to copy your answers on to the answer sheet during the 60 minutes, because you won't be given extra time to transfer the answers.

Each of the 40 questions receives one mark if the answer is correct, or zero if the answer is incorrect. The number of marks is then converted to an IELTS score on a nine-band scale.

All the questions will be about the information in the texts; however, the way you need to provide your answers can be different. Following the instructions precisely is a big part of success in IELTS.

How to write your answers in the IELTS Test

We recommend you write the answers in the question booklet, but reserve 5 minutes before the end of the test **to transfer them to the answer sheet**. Nothing written in the question booklet will be marked, and no extra time for copying answers will be given once your 60 minutes have ended.

You can write your answers in uppercase or lowercase letters, both ways are acceptable. Where possible, we recommend copying answer words directly from the passage, in order to avoid spelling errors.

For any question types with blanks to fill in, **use the words just as they are in the text**. There's no need to change them in any way, or to use synonyms.

Both British and American spelling versions are accepted. Whichever you adopt, please **make sure your spelling is correct**, because misspelled answers will get zero marks.

Correct grammar is important. Any answer with correct meaning but incorrect grammar will get zero marks. A common error, for example, is to use a singular form ('apple') instead of plural form ('apples'), or to use the wrong tense or verb form ('he go' instead of 'he goes'). **Ungrammatical answers will receive zero marks**.

 *Scan the QR code to access a **blank answer sheet** in the Treasure Chest or visit https://ielts-blog.com/treasure-chest*

Are you ready? Start the Entry Test now.

IELTS READING ENTRY TEST

READING PASSAGE 1

*You should spend about 20 minutes on **Questions 1 – 14**, which are based on Reading Passage 1 below.*

The Dancing Plague of 1518

A In July, over five hundred years ago, a strange mania descended upon the city of Strasbourg. Citizens, by the hundred, became unable to stop themselves dancing - in trance-like state for days until they became unconscious, or even died.

B In the busy horse market in Strasbourg in 1518, scores of people danced to pipes and drums. With the sun beating down on them they were seen spinning round and round in circles and shouting loudly. They probably looked like they were having a party, but closer inspection reveals a more unsettling scene. Their arms were waving around wildly, and their bodies convulsed as if in a spasm. They were saturated in sweat and their eyes looked glassy and distant. Blood was seeping from swollen feet into their leather boots. They were not party-goers but possessed by a dance mania. This mania tormented Strasbourg for a whole month during that summer, and became known as the 'dancing plague'. It was the most serious of more than ten similar contagions which had broken out along the Rhine and Moselle rivers since 1374; it was also the most documented.

C A doctor and alchemist, Paracelsus, visited Strasbourg eight years later and became fascinated by its causes. According to his *Opus Paramirum*, it all started with one woman. Frau Troffea had started dancing on July 14th on a narrow street outside her home. She probably had no musical accompaniment but simply began to dance, ignoring her husband's pleas to cease. She danced for hours until she collapsed in exhaustion. The next morning, she was up again and dancing despite badly swollen feet. By the third day all sorts of people - pilgrims, beggars, priests, nuns, porters were becoming affected by this strange spectacle. Frau Troffea's mania continued for nearly six days, at which point the local authorities intervened by sending her by wagon to a shrine at Saverne, a town thirty miles away.

D Some of those who had witnessed her performance started to mimic her, and within days there were more than thirty dancers, dancing so maniacally that only death could stop them. The more the numbers of dancers grew, the more desperate were the authorities to control them. The clergy believed that it was all the work of a vengeful St. Vitus, but the government officials listened instead to the physicians, who declared the dancing a natural disease caused by overheating of the blood. A typical recommendation for that condition in those days was to bleed the victims, but the doctors instead recommended that they should dance themselves free of the affliction. Local halls were transformed into dance floors and musicians were paid to play drums, fiddles, pipes and horns, with healthy dancers even brought in to provide encouragement.

E   This solution backfired terribly. Most of the spectators saw in the frenzied movements the magnitude of St.Vitus' fury, and as they saw themselves as sinners they felt compelled to join the mania. Within a month the plague had seized four hundred citizens. The authorities then ordered the dance floors to be taken down, and prohibited all dance and music until September. Any, less energetic, dancing was to take place out of public sight. In addition, the government ordered the worst afflicted to be taken on a three-day ride to the shrine of St. Vitus, where Frau Troffea had been 'cured'. There they were ritually cleansed of their illness. Word soon reached Strasbourg that this was having the desired effect, and more dancers were sent to the shrine in Saverne. Even so, by September, it is estimated that hundreds of people may have died of this 'dancing plague' through exhaustion.

F   If not an angry saint, what *did* cause the dancing plague? According to Paracelsus, Frau Troffea's marathon dance was a ploy to embarrass her husband. Upon seeing the success of her trick, other, often less respectable women began dancing to annoy their menfolk, too, accompanied by free and indecent thoughts. In the centuries that followed, certain historians argued instead that the dancing plagues were caused by a mind-altering mould found on damp grain, which could cause twitching, jerking and hallucinations. A modern historian, John Waller, has discredited this theory as this mould also restricts blood flow, so anyone poisoned by it simply could not dance for several days without a break. Waller's explanation of the plague is based more on the plight of the poor in Strasbourg. A succession of bad harvests, starvation and disease had induced within the people severe anxiety. This mental distress and suffering, compounded by the citizens' existing tendencies to be superstitious, found expression in hysterical dancing. Another historical researcher, Robert Bartholomew disagrees. He points out that records from the time suggest that the dancers were often pilgrims from other regions. Their behaviour he believes was designed to get spiritual favour and was to some degree consistent with Christian traditions, but had some unusual elements never before witnessed, including chanting names of previously unknown devils.

Is the 'dancing plague' so far-fetched? Contemporary, modern rave culture is perhaps not unlike plague dancing, though without the bloody feet and minus the religious beliefs.

Questions 1 – 5

Complete the flow chart below. Write **NO MORE THAN ONE WORD** from the text for each answer.

Write your answers in boxes 1 – 5 on your answer sheet.

Frau Troffea started dancing on July 14th 1518.

⇩

Six days later she was sent to Saverne by local officials to receive help.

⇩

The medical authorities suggested the community might (**1**) _____ itself of the mania by increasing opportunities to dance.

⇩

As a result, 400 citizens felt their sins (**2**) _____ them to mimic the manic dancing of Frau Troffea.

⇩

As the situation worsened, the authorities changed their policy and dancing in public was (**3**) _____.

⇩

The dancers who were most seriously (**4**) _____ were also sent to the shrine to be cured.

⇩

Even so, by September hundreds had died of total (**5**) _____.

IELTS Reading Section

Questions 6 – 9

*Answer the questions below. Write **NO MORE THAN TWO WORDS** from the text for each answer.*

*Write your answers in boxes **6 – 9** on your answer sheet.*

6 Apart from extreme fatigue what was the other, main repercussion of Frau Troffea's maniacal dancing?

7 What did local people think the Saint's reaction was to the frenzied dancing?

8 Whom did Frau Troffea try to annoy by dancing, according to one viewpoint?

9 What is the closest equivalent these days of the wild dancing of 1518?

Questions 10 – 14

*Look at the following beliefs (Questions **10 – 14**) and the list of people/groups below (**A – E**). Match each belief with the correct person/group, **A – E**.*

*Write the correct letter, **A – E** in boxes **10 – 14** on your answer sheet.*

A	Paracelsus
B	Waller
C	Bartholomew
D	Early Historians
E	Local doctors

10 The dancing plague was due to eating food which disturbed brain function.

11 The dancing plague was driven by religious beliefs.

12 The dancing plague was linked to social relationships.

13 The dancing plague was linked to a medical condition.

14 The dancing plague was largely psychological.

READING PASSAGE 2

*You should spend about 20 minutes on **Questions 15 – 27**, which are based on Reading Passage 2 below.*

Homelessness and Ageing in Canada

A   Like many countries, Canada has its share of people who not only have no home, but in addition are elderly citizens. Little attention has been given either to their unique needs or to analysing the effectiveness of approaches to their care, perhaps with the exception of Quebec, which has a national strategy.

B   There are problems with classifying types of homelessness, for example whether it is chronic or only temporary. Some researchers see chronic homelessness as involving three months of being without stable housing, while others opt for a period of one year as the cut-off point for that descriptor. Attempts to define homelessness among older people are even more limited, though it is generally seen as increasing. Sixty-five is the most commonly accepted marker for old age, but according to Morrison 2009, homeless people are around ten years older than that in terms of their mental and physical state of health. A study in Toronto in 2004 found that homeless people over fifty years of age subjectively viewed themselves as 'old'. This is unsurprising in view of the fact that the average age of death for a homeless person in Canada is around thirty-nine.

C   There are various pathways that show how people end up being homeless. The rising cost of housing is an obvious one, as is less availability of jobs, simple poverty, and loss of social networks. Government policies that limit eligibility for financial benefits are also a factor. Put together, these factors often give rise to a gradual decline into homelessness. Other risk factors include a history of mental illness (Barack and Cohen 2003), traumatic life changes such as deaths in the family, worsened by limited family networks. Native Americans are also over-represented in the homeless population. Research literature suggests that becoming homeless for the first time in later life, rather than lifelong homelessness, is an increasing proportion of the total.

D   There are differences also between men and women, with homeless men outnumbering women by a ratio of four to one, though that ratio narrows among older age groups. It is thought, however, that the incidence of homeless women is under-reported as they are generally less visible, and more often homeless through poverty or escaping abusive relationships than through loss of job or mental health issues. It is clear, though, that other health issues do accompany the hardship of homelessness. The most frequently reported health problems in Toronto were arthritis, poor vision, dental problems and back problems, while in the US, one study found that heart problems, lung disease, diabetes and arthritis were prominent.

E   Drug and alcohol abuse is often seen as a common factor in homelessness, but the literature on substance use in older people is not conclusive. Some studies have found that substance use decreases with age; other studies suggest that younger and older homeless people are equally likely to report alcohol abuse. Earlier research suggested that older people were less likely to report drug use, but later studies indicate an upward trend in drug-taking among the older homeless.

F   In light of this distressing overall picture, what do homeless people need? Obviously, whatever their age or gender, they need housing, income, food and health care, but older homeless also have special needs such as safety and access to specialised health and social services, as they are more likely to have mental and physical problems not treatable in shelters with limited resources. As older homeless people often report discriminatory treatment in health care settings there is a need, too, for medical staff to develop more sensitive responses. Problems with finding appropriate government services is another barrier to adequate support. Language problems sometimes become a barrier to accessing housing and financial benefits for which older homeless people may qualify. Safety is also an important need for the older homeless person. Many of them encounter violence on the streets and in shelters because their poor health makes them an easy target.

G   Homelessness among different groups of older people is thus a significant example of social marginalisation and is likely to rise not just in Canada but in many other countries across the world. There need to be accurate estimates of the numbers of older people without homes and their diversity, and a political agenda to improve affordable housing and appropriate resources and supports.

Questions 15 – 20

Passage 2 has 7 paragraphs **A – G**. Which paragraph contains the following information?

Write your answers in boxes **15 – 20** on your answer sheet.

15   Inadequate health make the older homeless more open to physical assault.

16   Researchers do not have standardised definitions of various dimensions of homelessness.

17   The descent into homelessness results in part from inadequate social and family connections.

18   Older homeless people have a health profile normally associated with even much older people.

19   Homeless people sometimes have difficulty locating various state resources.

20   Politicians need to make housing more financially available.

Questions 21 – 24

Do the following statements agree with the views of the writer of the text?

In boxes **21 – 24** on your answer sheet write:

YES	if the statement agrees with the writer's views
NO	if the statement doesn't agree with the writer's views
NOT GIVEN	if it is impossible to say what the writer thinks about this

21   The descent into homelessness occurs suddenly once causal factors multiply.

22   Because women are more difficult to trace, the larger numbers of older male homeless may be misleading.

23   The incidence of substance abuse among older homeless people is mixed, with no clear picture.

24   Older homeless people are more sensitive than younger homeless and need to be treated in specialist hospitals.

IELTS Reading Section

Questions 25 – 27

Complete the notes below. Write **NO MORE THAN ONE WORD** from the text for each answer.

Write your answers in boxes **25 – 27** on your answer sheet.

What is 'older' homelessness?

- Can be short-term or chronic depending on length of time.
- 'Older' can mean over 65, but homeless over 50s, (**25**) _____, can perceive themselves as old.
- Poor health adds ten years to actual age.

Pathways into homelessness

- Various life events - poverty, expensive housing, no jobs, loss of social networks.
- Not qualifying for government (**26**) _____.
- Background of poor physical and mental health or substance abuse.

Measures needed to improve the situation

- Provision of housing, income and health and social care.
- Carers for older homeless to be more (**27**) _____.
- Help with safety issues such as violence in the street or in shelters.

READING PASSAGE 3

*You should spend about 20 minutes on **Questions 28 – 40**, which are based on Reading Passage 3 below.*

The Problems of Microplastics in the Oceans

It is estimated that 230 million tons of plastic were produced worldwide in 2009, accounting for 8% of global oil production. Of course, apart from its durability, there are significant social benefits of plastics, but the disposal of plastic is problematic, a situation exacerbated by the multiple use of throw-away 'user' plastics, like packaging material. Some plastic is recycled, but the majority ends up in landfill where it may take centuries to decompose. Of especial concern are plastics that enter the marine environment due to indiscriminate disposal.

Up to 10% of all plastics end up in the oceans where they accumulate, endure and cause damage. Large plastic debris, called 'macroplastics' have long been researched - they present both an aesthetic issue with economic implications for tourism, and a hazard to marine industries like shipping, energy production and fishing, resulting in entanglement or damage to equipment. Even worse, they lead to the injury and death of marine birds, mammals and fish due to ingestion and entanglement, and also the smothering of the sea bed which prevents gas exchange. In recent years there has been increasing concern about 'microplastics' - tiny plastic granules used in cosmetics and air blasting, and small fragments formed from the breakdown of macroplastics. These tiny particles are widespread in the oceans and potentially harm animal and plant life there. They are capable of sticking to other waterborne pollutants and of releasing toxic plastic ingredients, often into the marine food chain where they accumulate.

Microplastics have different sizes which often make it difficult for data comparison. Primary microplastics are only of microscopic size - found typically in facial cleaners, hand cleansers and other cosmetic products that previously used natural ingredients like pumice and oatmeal. In air blasting they are used to scrub boat hulls, or to remove rust and paint. Secondary microplastics are formed when larger plastic debris breaks down under the effects of wave action, sunlight and UV radiation. This more commonly and more rapidly occurs on beaches rather than in the oceans themselves, where decomposition times are prolonged.

The microplastics enter the oceans from a variety of sources. Plastic litter from rivers and wastewater is the main one, given that about half the world's population lives within 80 kilometres of the coast. The wind also blows waste offshore and into the ocean. Waste cosmetic products can enter waterways through domestic or industrial drainage systems. Macroplastics can be trapped or filtered, but microplastics pass through filtration systems. Increased water volumes in rivers following storms accelerate the movement of microplastics. Tourism also makes plastic pollution worse, as does discarded plastic fishing gear, like nylon netting or fishing line.

Measuring plastic debris in the oceans is complicated by the sheer size of the oceans, compared with the small size of the plastics being assessed. Nevertheless, the main methods used include beachcombing, sampling of sediment, sampling live creatures or plants, observation surveys, and trawling the sea with nets. The simplest method is probably beachcombing, but this technique makes it difficult to measure the level of plastic debris in the ocean itself.

Plastic litter is present across the globe and can be transported vast distances by currents and winds, ending up in remote, otherwise clean locations such as mid-ocean islands or the poles, and even in the ocean depths. A high proportion of plastic debris ends up in ocean gyres - the systems of rotating currents in the main oceans. The North Pacific gyre has sometimes been called 'plastic soup'.

Looking into the ocean depths, it can be seen that plastics either float, are semi-buoyant or sink, depending on composition, density and shape. Sometimes microbes attach to the plastics, generating algae which increase density and weight of the debris, and reducing buoyancy. Research in the Netherlands by Von Franeker into the plastic debris inside the stomachs of marine birds such as fulmars shows that between the 1980s and 2000, average consumption of plastics by these ocean-foraging seabirds doubled from 15 to 30 fragments per bird, but has stabilised. More recent studies by Claessens et al. in 2011 suggest that microplastic concentrations have steadily increased over the past two decades. Conclusions are made difficult by lack of studies specifically considering trends of plastic levels, and by varying sampling methodologies, and unstandardised definitions of microplastic size.

What is clear is that microplastics have the potential to be ingested by all sorts of marine creatures throughout the food chain, starting with tiny plankton and ranging up to birds, crustaceans and fish. As plastics break down chemically, sea creatures can ingest toxic chemicals that can disrupt natural processes such as mobility, reproduction, physical development, and also lead to cancers. Much more research is needed as fundamental issues remain unresolved. The overall situation seems alarming, but it still remains unclear whether the ingestion of microplastics alone will result in adverse health effects or whether these particles are passed up the food chain. More studies need to be undertaken to trace the transfer of toxic chemicals via ingestion of microplastics by marine creatures.

Questions 28 – 33

Do the following statements agree with the information given in the text?
In boxes **28 – 33** on your answer sheet write:

> **TRUE** if the statement agrees with the information
> **FALSE** if the statement contradicts the information
> **NOT GIVEN** if there is no information on this

28 Plastics end up in the oceans through planned disposal measures

29 Macroplastics are known to be more harmful than microplastics.

30 Microplastics can adhere to harmful, non-living substances in the oceans.

31 Beachcombing is the most statistically effective method of measuring ocean levels of plastic waste.

32 The rotational movement of ocean gyres concentrates plastic waste in dense areas of water.

33 It is uncertain whether sea creatures develop health problems simply by swallowing microplastics.

Questions 34-38

Complete the sentences below. Write **NO MORE THAN ONE WORD** from the text for each answer.

Write your answers in boxes **34-38** on your answer sheet.

(**34**) _____ microplastics derive from beauty items that previously used natural substances.

Macroplastics can be caught or trapped in flowing rivers whereas microplastics, being so small, can evade (**35**) _____.

Microplastic waste is everywhere, even ending up in the middle of the oceans on pristine and (**36**) _____ islands.

Tiny living organisms sometimes glue themselves to plastics in the ocean, lessening their (**37**) _____.

Measuring plastic fragments in birds' (**38**) _____ enables assessment of increases in their ingestion across time.

Questions 39 and 40

*Choose the correct letter **A**, **B**, **C** or **D**. Write the correct letter in boxes **39 - 40** on your answer sheet.*

39   According to the first paragraph the writer's central view seems to be that plastics are

    A   simply harmful and a growing problem to the land and to the water far into the future.

    B   a good thing for society despite minor environmental problems on land and in the sea.

    C   largely recycled and the small percentage that ends up in landfill, breaks down easily.

    D   increasingly used, but inadequate disposal creates long-term problems on land and to marine life.

40   According to the final paragraph, the writer's central summarising point seems to be

    A   More research is needed to reduce the uncertainty around the effects of toxic microplastics on marine life.

    B   The presence of microplastics in the oceans is alarming and dangerous, and needs to change.

    C   Sea creatures of all sizes which consume microplastics will probably get cancer and develop other health issues.

    D   More research is needed into ingestion along the whole marine food chain to aid knowledge.

Score, Review then Practise

Score your Entry Test

 Now you have finished the Entry Test, **check the answers**, located in the IELTS Answers section **at the end of this book**.

Add up your total score out of 40. Remember that your spelling has to be correct, and your answers must be in the correct place.

Review

Once you know your total score, go back to your answers and try to identify the kinds of errors you made, and the way you proceeded through the texts and questions.

- Which passage was the most difficult, and why?
- Which question types did you find the most difficult?
- Were your spellings accurate?
- Did you spend about the same amount of time on each passage?
- Did you have enough time to finish? If not, what were your problems?
- How did you cope with words you didn't understand?

Use questions like those above to build a personal profile of your performance.

Practise

Once your review is complete, move on to the next section of this book and practise all the question types used in IELTS Reading, especially the types that are still difficult for you.

Boost Your Performance

For any reading activities that you still find troublesome, check the useful test strategies given on Page 75 and ways to solve common test-taking problems. Then try those challenging reading activities again, and change any of your answers that seem wrong.

READING TEST PRACTICE

WHAT'S INSIDE:

- **Practise the Question Types**
- **Boost Your Performance**

IELTS Reading Section

Practise the Question Types

QUESTION TYPE 1 — Matching Paragraph Headings

In this question type you need to select the appropriate heading to each paragraph of text. Not every heading on the list may be used.

To match headings more quickly, **the best strategy** is to go in the order of paragraphs, not in the order of headings. Go to paragraph 1, look for a suitable heading in the list, then go to paragraph 2, look for a suitable heading, and so on.

Complete this Reading activity to practise an example of matching paragraph headings.

 The answers to all Activities are located in the IELTS Answers section at the end of this book.

Activity 1

The reading passage on the following page, **AUSTRALIA's DAM STORY (Part 1)**, has five paragraphs, **A–E**. Choose the correct heading for paragraphs **B–E** from the list of headings below.

Write the correct number **i–ix** below. Choose each heading once only.

List of Headings

i	Problems in Paradise?
ii	Benefits outstrip problems
iii	Development of dams in Australia
iv	The importance of water to humans
v	How to solve problems with dams
vi	**Australia's rainfall profile [Example]**
vii	The role of science in the planning of dams
viii	Disadvantages outweigh gains
ix	Meeting Sydney's water needs

1	Paragraph A	vi [Example]
2	Paragraph B	_____
3	Paragraph C	_____
4	Paragraph D	_____
5	Paragraph E	_____

AUSTRALIA's DAM STORY (Part 1)

Paragraph A
Measured across the continent, Australia receives an average of only 465 mm of rainfall a year, compared with Europe's 640 mm and Asia's 600 mm. High evaporation allows just 12 per cent of its rainfall to run off and reach waterways. Even so, there's enough water for everyone—but it's seldom in the right place at the right time.

Paragraph B
European settlers solved this problem with dams. The first two—Yan Yean outside Melbourne and Lake Parramatta, Sydney—were completed in 1857. Dam building continued steadily until after World War II, when it accelerated. Today, 500 large (more than 15 m high) dams store a total of 93,957 gigalitres (Sydney Harbour holds about 562 GL). There are also countless smaller dams, called weirs, on most Australian rivers—8000 in the Murray-Darling Basin alone—and more than 2 million farm dams.

Paragraph C
Large dams bring quick benefits. They can provide water and electricity, mitigate flooding and create beautiful lakes. But they also have adverse impacts. The first are those on people living in the way of a dam and its lake. They may need to be moved, causing families and communities to fragment. The lake may flood farmland or natural landscape. Many of the drowned river's plants and animals fail to adapt to lake conditions. Alien fish species, introduced into the reservoir accidentally, or for recreational fishing, may further alter the biological make-up of water life, and weeds and algae may thrive in the nutrient-rich water. Downstream, changes in the river's flow and water quality usually cause irreversible effects, often down to the river mouth and beyond. Fish migration and reproduction, siltation and salinity in deltas are altered.

Paragraph D
Once upon a time, these adverse impacts—some of which take years to manifest—weren't really considered before a dam was built. The human need for water, for drinking or to grow food, took precedence. Some people believe they should still. But over recent decades, science has deepened our understanding of natural systems, which we now know can't be broken into discrete pieces, some of which can be exploited and others not. This has given rise to the idea that the environment itself is a legitimate water consumer, with attendant needs and rights. All this calls for careful study of a river's state and function before it's dammed.

Paragraph E
Australia's newest megadam straddles a gentle valley on the Burnett River, 260 km north-west of Brisbane. Apart from a soupy stain low on its upstream face, the concrete is spotless and dazzles the eye under the sharp Queensland sun. This is Paradise Dam, completed in 2005. Impressive though it may be, Paradise, like other large dams, is a mix of good points and bad. For some people, the bad prevail. High among the complaints has been that the rationale behind it was political. Then there are the potential environmental impacts downstream, especially around the river's mouth in Hervey Bay, which worry people such as commercial fishers and tourism operators.

Source: *Australian Geographic, Issue 89 (Jan–Mar, 2007)*

IELTS Reading Section

QUESTION TYPE 2   Multiple Choice Questions

In this question type you need to select the correct answer from three or four options. Sometimes you may be required to select more than one option.

The best strategy is to read the question and find the paragraph that is discussing the same topic. If the right answer is not immediately visible, begin eliminating the wrong answer options one by one, based on the information in the paragraph.

Use this fact to help you: the answers to multiple choice questions are located sequentially in the text. If you've found the answer to question 1, and the answer to question 3, then the answer to question 2 will probably be between them.

Complete this Reading activity

Activity 2

The reading passage on the previous page, **AUSTRALIA's DAM STORY (Part 1)**, has five paragraphs, **A–E**.

1   Using ONLY **paragraph C** of the text, choose the appropriate letter A, B, C, or D.

   One of the problems of dams is that:
   - **A**   new plant species may change the biological balance
   - **B**   they cause more drowning
   - **C**   they lead to changes in salt levels in water further up river
   - **D**   weeds and algae can't survive as easily

2   Using ONLY **paragraph D** of the text, choose the appropriate letter A, B, C, or D.

   According to the passage, the negative features of dams:
   - **A**   were originally given precedence over the demand for water
   - **B**   were at first taken into account before construction
   - **C**   have given rise to more sensitivity about the environment
   - **D**   have led to national studies of river care

3   Using ONLY **paragraph E** of the text, choose the appropriate letter A, B, C, or D.

   According to the passage, Paradise Dam:
   - **A**   has been entirely beneficial
   - **B**   is situated beyond a valley
   - **C**   has provided environmental advantages for tourists
   - **D**   may have been built for political reasons

QUESTION TYPE 3   Summary Completion

This question type involves writing missing words in the gaps. Sometimes you will need to copy words from the text, other times you may be given a list of words to choose from.

The best strategy is to try and guess what kind of word is missing. Even if you can't guess the meaning of the word, you can still guess whether it's, say, a verb, a noun, or an adjective, by looking at the words around the gap.

Once you know the kind of word that's missing, it is easier to find it in the text or in the list of words in a box.

While reading the sentence around the gap, also note what it's about, and use that information when you're scanning the text to locate the paragraph where the answer might be.

In the selected paragraph look for words of the same type that could go in the gap. If a verb is missing—look at verbs, if an adjective is missing—look at adjectives, and so on. After you've found the best candidate for the gap, always read the whole sentence, to make sure it makes sense and that grammatically it is correct.

Hint: If you find yourself changing the words from the text, or their form, before writing them in the gap, it means that you've got the wrong answer. In question types such as sentence completion or summary completion you should be able to find the correct answer right in the text, and copy it as is, without changing a thing.

The second best strategy is elimination. For example, when you have a list of words to choose from, after you've used most of the options and only have a few left it will be easier to eliminate the wrong ones, and pick the right ones.

Complete this Reading activity

Activity 3

Complete the summary below based on paragraphs **C** and **D** ONLY of the text **AUSTRALIA's DAM STORY (Part 1)**. Choose **NO MORE THAN ONE WORD** from the text for each answer.

Dams have benefits and drawbacks. For example, they provide water and **1** _____ but those residing in the dam's path may have to be **2** _____ . The reservoir may **3** _____ agricultural land, and biological changes may include unwanted fish species. In recent years better understanding of nature has been helped by **4** _____ . The environment is now seen as having rights just like every other **5** _____ of water.

IELTS Reading Section

QUESTION TYPE 4 — Diagram, Map Or Plan Labelling

This question type involves writing short descriptions of up to three words and/or a number for parts of a drawing.

The best strategy is to look at the diagram, map or plan, and then scan the text to locate the relevant paragraph. Once you found the correct location in the text, read closely to find the answers.

Complete this Reading activity

Activity 4

Look at the diagrams of types of dams (**A–D**) and read each dam description below. Label each description with the appropriate letter (**A–D**) based on the text **AUSTRALIA's DAM STORY (Part 1)**.

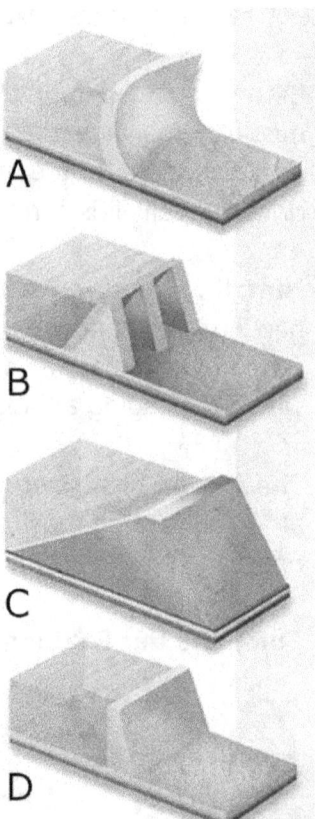

Dam Type	Description of Dams
_____	**Embankment dams** use a long-sloped, massive volume of rock, gravel and sand, with the finest materials in the centre to form a waterproof core.
_____	**Buttress dams** have 45-degree walls that transfer the force downwards.
_____	**Gravity dams** are thick, massive structures with a vertical face that can hold back enormous amounts of water under their own weight.
_____	**Arch dams** have curved sides which redirect a lot of pressure to the valley sides.

QUESTION TYPE 5 — Yes/No/Not Given (Identifying Writer's Views)

In this question type you will be given a list of statements and asked to decide whether each statement agrees with the author's claim or view, contradicts it, or there is no reference to it in the text.

If the statement clearly agrees with text, the answer is Yes, if the statement explicitly contradicts the text, the answer is No, and if the statement says something that the text doesn't say, it's Not Given.

Questions of this type may feel harder, because apart from testing your English they test your logical thinking as well. Don't worry, it gets easier with practice.

The best strategy is to scan the text quickly to find the relevant paragraph, and then read in detail. Check whether or not **the text says the same thing as the statement, in different words**. If so, **the answer is Yes**. When **the text says the complete opposite to the statement, the answer is No**. If the information in the text **neither the same nor opposite to the statement, the answer is Not Given**.

Use this fact to help you: the answers to Yes/No/Not Given questions are located sequentially in the text. If you've found the answer to question 1, and the answer to question 3, then the answer to question 2 will probably be between them.

Complete this Reading activity

Activity 5

Refer to the reading passage on the following page, **AUSTRALIA's DAM STORY (Part 2)**.

Do the following statements reflect the claims of the writer in **paragraph A** of the text? Write:

YES	if the statement reflects the claims of the writer
NO	if the statement contradicts the claims of the writer
NOT GIVEN	if it is impossible to say what the writer thinks about this

1   The deteriorating situation of the lungfish has stimulated public support.   _____

2   The habitat of the lungfish is now limited primarily to only two rivers.   _____

3   Biologists officially consider the lungfish to be an endangered species.   _____

4   The breeding grounds of the lungfish have no legal protection.   _____

AUSTRALIA's DAM STORY (Part 2)

Paragraph A   THREATENED SPECIES

But nothing has galvanised public opinion more than the plight of the endangered Australian, or Queensland, lungfish. Among the last of a group that lived 400 million years ago, this once-abundant fish is restricted mostly to the Burnett and Mary rivers. Biologists believe Paradise Dam has had, and will have, serious consequences for it. A fishway was installed to comply with the Commonwealth's Environmental Protection and Biodiversity Conservation Act (EPBC Act), which lists the lungfish as endangered. The Act requires the fish's spawning and nursery habitat to be preserved. Jean Joss, Professor of Biology at Sydney's Macquarie University, says lungfish spawn in slow-flowing shallows with plenty of native water plants. "When it [Paradise dam] is full, it will have permanently destroyed 42 km of lungfish spawning/nursery grounds," she says.

Paragraph B   GROWTH AND THIRST

Declining water consumption in most of Australia has stalled dam-building in recent years. But not in south-east Queensland. There, the population is set to soar from 2.8 million today to 5 million in 2050, and water consumption is expected to climb with it. The region mirrors not only what has happened historically elsewhere in Australia but also what's happening across the world. Look here and you see humanity's past and its future. South-east Queensland consumes about 440,000 ML a year. The Queensland Government says that by 2050 the region will need 330,000–490,000 ML more, even with water restrictions.

Paragraph C   ALTERNATIVE OPTIONS FOR MEETING WATER DEMAND

Prodded by drought but committed to economic growth, the government has assembled a mix of measures to provide the extra water. Among them are recycling, desalination, raising some existing dams and building two new ones – Traveston Crossing on the Mary River, and Wyaralong nearer to Brisbane.

Paragraph D   THE MARY RIVER DAM PROPOSALS

Queensland Water Infrastructure (QWI) Pty Ltd would build the dam in two stages. Stage 1, due by 2020 and costing $1.6 billion, would flood 3000 ha of farmland and 334 properties; Stage 2, due after 2040, would raise the total cost to $2.5 billion and flood an extra 7135 ha and 265 properties. The dam wall would be made of RCC (Roller Compacted Concrete) at its western end and would merge with an earth-and-rock embankment.

Since one aim of the dam is to limit flooding in Gympie, 20 km to the north, the spillway would have six floodgates. QWI aims to build the dam to Stage 2 height immediately so that the only extra work needed later to raise the water level by another 8.5 m would be the fitting of higher gates. As with Paradise dam, there was talk of political expediency, but the government insisted the looming water crisis allowed no choice.

Paragraph E   SATISFYING THE ENVIRONMENTAL IMPACTS OF THE MARY RIVER DAM

In its Environmental Impact Statement (EIS) on the project, published in October 2007, QWI maintained the dam was the cheapest option offering maximum water returns. On the environment it was upbeat, saying downstream impacts would be negligible and that it could manage the effects around the dam's footprint such that wildlife might even be better off than now. As in the Burnett, the lungfish is central here. But in the Mary it's joined by the Mary River cod and the Mary River turtle. Since all are legally protected under national environmental legislation, the project needs federal approval. A decision based on the final Environmental Impact Statement is due soon.

QUESTION TYPE 6   Matching Information

In this question type you will need to find a paragraph that has the information in the question, or match statements to certain items from a list, or categorise features.

The best strategy is to quickly scan the text to find the relevant paragraph and then read in detail to make sure the information in it matches the statement.

Complete this Reading activity

Activity 6

Refer to the reading passage on the previous page, **AUSTRALIA's DAM STORY (Part 2)**.

Which **paragraph (B, C, D or E)** above contains the following information?

1   Measures for accommodating likely increases in demand for water.   _____

2   Data illustrating current and projected water demand in Queensland.   _____

3   Cost benefit gains and low projected impact of the Mary River Dam.   _____

4   The aquatic life affected by the proposed new dam.   _____

5   The likely timing and sequencing of dam construction.   _____

IELTS Reading Section

QUESTION TYPE 7   Form/Note Completion

In this question type you will need to write some missing words in the gaps. The words you write in the blanks must come from the text without any change to their form. It is similar to Summary Completion, but instead of a summary you may be given a set of bulleted notes, a form or a table.

The best strategy is to read the words around the gap and understand what kind of information is missing. Then scan the text to locate the relevant paragraph and once you get to it, read in detail to find the answer.

Hint: If you find yourself changing the words from the text, or their form, before writing them in the gap, it means that you've got the wrong answer. In question types such as sentence completion or summary completion you should be able to find the correct answer right in the text, and copy it as is, without changing a thing.

Complete this Reading activity

Activity 7

Using only **paragraph D** of the text **AUSTRALIA's DAM STORY (Part 2)**, complete the notes below.

Choose **NO MORE THAN THREE WORDS AND/OR A NUMBER** from the text for each answer.

• Overall cost of the dam = **1** _____

• Reduction of **2** _____ = a goal of building the dam

• **3** _____ to be fitted to enable increase in water level

• Government claimed no alternative due to approach of **4** _____

QUESTION TYPE 8   Matching Features

This question type involves finding descriptions in the text and matching them to people's names or places on a given list.

The best strategy is to scan the text for the person's name / place and then read in detail to find which of the descriptions matches each person / place.

Complete this Reading activity

Activity 8

Which of the individuals mentioned in **AUSTRALIA's DAM STORY (Part 3)** on the following page has these points of view?

Write **A** (for Professor **A**rthington), **I** (for Kevin **I**ngersole) and P (for Glenda **P**ickersgill).

Which person (**A**, **I** or **P**) believes that

1   ...most printed material about the dam is really an attempt to promote it?   _____

2   ...a large amount of the available documentation outlines the difficulties
    experienced by river life resulting from dams?   _____

3   ...it is vital to distribute material about the dam to the local population.   _____

AUSTRALIA's DAM STORY (Part 3)

For Mary Valley residents, nothing will ever repair damage already caused to families and communities by the dam's announcement and Queensland Water Infrastructure's (QWI) purchase of properties in the dam's footprint. QWI acknowledges that stress, depression, community disintegration and deep mistrust have resulted but says not everyone has suffered.

By late 2007, QWI had reached sale agreements for 65 per cent of the land it needs before it can build the new dam. Many people who sold have leased back their former properties and may continue to live on them for a time. One who hasn't sold is Glenda Pickersgill. Glenda breeds cattle about 1 km upstream of the proposed dam site. Her house and land would vanish under water at Stage 1. The farm has been in Glenda's family for 30 years and she has owned it for 20. Glenda was devastated by the Queensland Government's announcement about planning to build a new dam.

As a member of the Save the Mary River Coordinating Group, an anti-dam residents' coalition, Glenda has thrown all her energy into getting information about the project into the community and rallying support for the campaign against it. Anti-dam protest signs dot the Mary Valley. The signs cluster in greatest quantity and variety at Kandanga's old railway station, used these days only by a historic steam train. There, an airy weatherboard shed has become the headquarters and public information centre of the Save the Mary River Coordinating Group.

The group's chairman, Kevin Ingersole, 63, is a dynamic, semi-retired management consultant who bought a property in the valley five years ago. At Stage 1 he would lose much of his land. Kevin is bitter but, like Glenda, he diverts his emotions into action. He considers the Environmental Impact Statement (EIS) and its associated documents to be a magnificent sales pitch for building a dam, and claims that the government has not demonstrated that the proposed dam at Traveston Crossing is the best long-term solution for south-east Queensland's water-supply needs.

QWI's documents certainly attempt to build a convincing case for the dam's long-term economic importance to the region, emphasising increases in gross regional product, employment and business potential. QWI also claims that the dam's long-term cost will be more than $200 million less than the 'next best' water-supply alternative, a desalination plant. What irks Mary Valley residents most, however, is that water from the proposed reservoir would be pumped out of the area. Of the lake's 153,000 ML at Stage 1, 70,000 ML would go out every year. At Stage 2 the lake would hold 570,000 ML and would yield up to 150,000 ML a year. Professor Angela Arthington says the environmental consequences of such extraction, together with the flooding of a shallow valley, are predictable because they characterise all megadams in similar landscapes. She believes that thousands of publications document the adverse effects of dams on river and estuarine ecosystems.

IELTS Reading Section

| QUESTION TYPE 9 | True/False/Not Given (Identifying Information) |

In this question type you will be given a list of statements and asked to decide whether each statement agrees with the text, contradicts it, or there is no reference to it in the text.

The best strategy is to quickly scan the text to find the relevant paragraph, and then read in detail. Check whether or not the text says the same thing as the statement, in different words. If so, the answer is True. When the text says the complete opposite to the statement, the answer is False. If the information in the text neither the same nor opposite to the statement, the answer is Not Given.

Use this fact to help you: the answers to True/False/Not Given questions are located sequentially in the text. If you've found the answer to question 1, and the answer to question 3, then the answer to question 2 will probably be between them.

Complete this Reading activity

Activity 9

Do the following statements agree with the information given in the text on the previous page, **AUSTRALIA's DAM STORY (Part 3)**?

Answer:

    TRUE   if the statement agrees with the information
    FALSE   if the statement contradicts the information
    NOT GIVEN if there is no information on this

1. QWI accepts that social problems resulting from purchase of properties have affected everyone. _____

2. People who have sold their land to QWI may not leave it for some time. _____

3. The majority of the anti-dam signs are near Kandanga Railway station. _____

4. The EIS discusses the sale of Kevin Ingersole's land to the government. _____

5. QWI's documents predict that regional wealth will grow. _____

6. QWI consider that the dam will be less expensive than a desalination plant. _____

7. People who live in Mary Valley are annoyed about the likely loss of water from their area when the reservoir is in operation. _____

8. Professor Arthington is unsure about the environmental outcomes likely to arise as a result of the new dam. _____

IELTS Reading Section

QUESTION TYPE 10   Matching Sentence Endings

In this question type you will need to complete sentences according to the information in the text. There is a list of sentence endings provided in a box for you to choose from. There may be more sentence endings than sentences.

The best strategy is to read the sentence and then scan the text to locate the relevant paragraph. Once you get to it, read in detail to find the answer and then read all the sentence endings in the box, to find the correct ending.

Complete this Reading activity

Activity 10

Refer to the text **AUSTRALIA's DAM STORY (Part 3)**.

Choose the best endings for sentences **1–4** from the **List of Options A–H** in the box below.

1. After the QWI announcement, many Mary Valley residents _____

2. Glenda Pickersgill is likely to lose her land and property _____

3. Five years ago, the chairman of the Save the Mary River Coordinating Group _____

4. Angela Arthington believes that megadams cause flooding of valleys _____

	List of Options
A	to her family during the next thirty years
B	purchased a valley property
C	which are extracted during construction
D	suffered traumatic psychological effects
E	can be repaired by avoiding all the damage
F	was a full-time management consultant
G	during Stage 1 of the dam's development
H	that are characteristically shallow

QUESTION TYPE 11   Sentence Completion

In this question type you need to complete a sentence according to the text.

The best strategy is to read the sentence and then scan the text to locate the relevant paragraph. Once you get to it, read in detail to find the answer and then complete the sentence using words from the text. Re-read the finished sentence to ensure it is grammatically correct, because if the grammar is faulty, your answer is incorrect.

Hint: If you find yourself changing the words from the text, or their form for them to fit in the sentence, it means that you've got the wrong answer. In this question type you should be able to find the correct answer right in the text, and copy it as is, without changing a thing.

Complete this Reading activity to practise an example of sentence completion questions

Activity 11

Refer to the text **AUSTRALIA's DAM STORY (Part 3)**.

Complete the sentences below. Choose **NO MORE THAN TWO WORDS OR A NUMBER** from the text for each answer.

1   Glenda Pickersgill was _____ when she heard of the government's dam-building plans.

2   Glenda is trying hard to build _____ for the anti-dam protest group.

3   Kevin Ingersole remains unconvinced that the proposed dam is the optimal _____ to regional water needs.

4   At Stage 2 _____ would be extracted from the lake annually.

IELTS Reading Section

QUESTION TYPE 12 — Short-Answer Questions

You need to answer this question type using one, two or three words and/or a number. You are not required to write a complete sentence, and it is important that you don't write more words than the instructions specify.

The best strategy is to read the sentence and then scan the text to locate the relevant paragraph. Once you get to it, read in detail to find the answer. Re-read your answer to make sure you haven't written more words than you are allowed.

Complete this Reading activity

Activity 12

Refer to the text **AUSTRALIA's DAM STORY (Part 3)**.

Answer the questions below. Choose **NO MORE THAN TWO WORDS AND/OR A NUMBER** from the text for each answer.

1. What has been the irreparable outcome of QWI's property purchase on the whole community?
   _____

2. In what direction is Glenda's land relative to the proposed dam?
   _____

3. In what type of dwelling does the Save the Mary River Group have its central office?
   _____

4. Although he remains proactive, how does Kevin Ingersole feel?
   _____

5. In financial terms, what is the economic benefit of a dam compared with a desalination plant?
   _____

QUESTION TYPE 13   Flow Chart/Table Completion

In this question type you need to fill in the blank table cells or diagram blocks.

The best strategy is to look at the table / diagram and scan the text to locate the relevant paragraph. Often the information for the diagram can be found in a specific location in the text such as one or two *consecutive* paragraphs. Once you get to it, read in detail to fill in the gaps.

Complete this Reading activity

Activity 13

Complete the diagram below based on the text '**How evaporated milk is produced**', on the following page.

Choose **NO MORE THAN TWO WORDS** from the text for each answer.

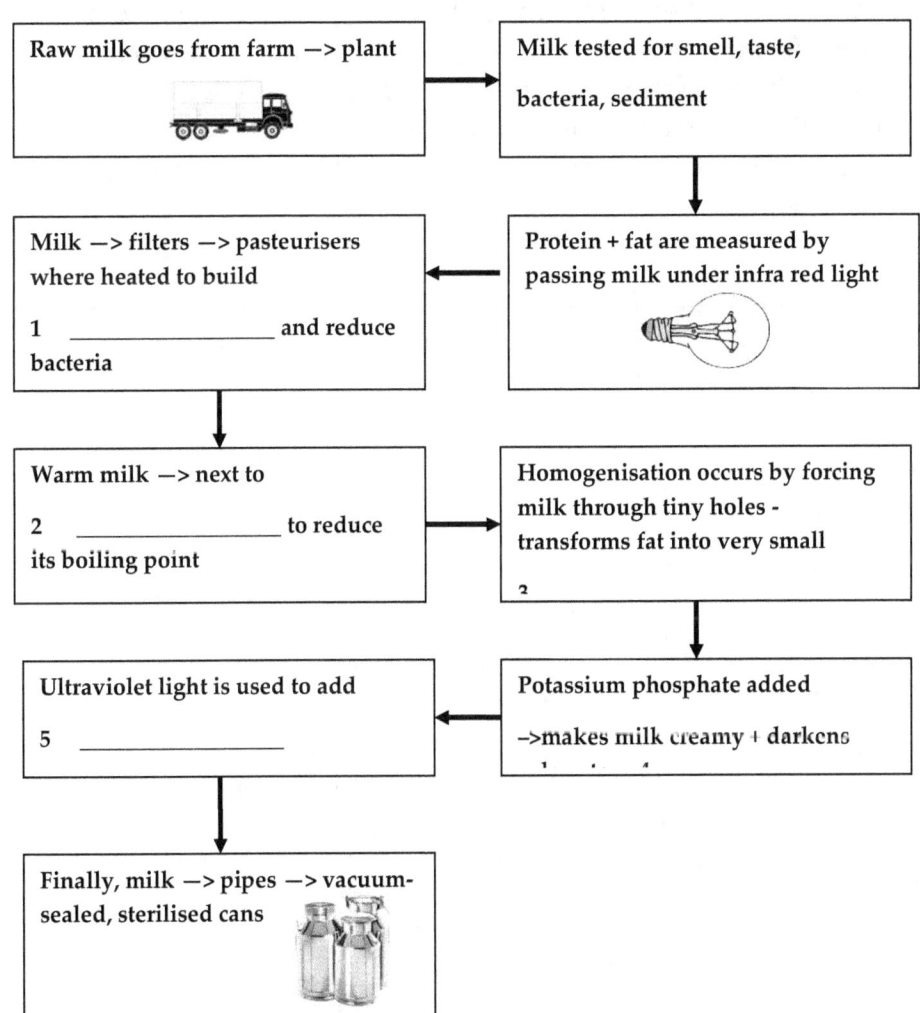

How evaporated milk is produced

First, the raw milk is transported from the dairy farm to the plant in refrigerated tank trucks. At the plant, the milk is tested for odour, taste, bacteria, sediment, and the composition of milk protein and milk fat. The composition of protein and fat is measured by passing the milk under highly sensitive infrared lights. After this, the milk is piped through filters and into the pasteurizers where it is quickly heated in one of two ways: the High Temperature Short Time method (HTST) subjects the milk to temperatures of 71.6°C for 15 seconds; the Ultra High Temperature (UHT) method heats the milk to 138°C for two seconds. The two methods increase the milk's stability, and decrease both the chance of coagulation during storage, and the bacteria levels. Next, the warm milk is piped to an evaporator. Through the process of vacuum evaporation, (a pressure lower than atmospheric pressure) the boiling point of the milk is lowered to 40–45°C. As a result, the milk is concentrated to 30–40% solids and has little or no cooked flavour. The milk is then homogenized by forcing it under high pressure through tiny holes. This breaks down the fat globules into minute particles, improving its colour and stability. Pre-measured amounts of a stabilizing salt, such as potassium phosphate, are added to the milk to make it smooth and creamy. This stabilization causes the milk to turn a pale tan. Finally, the milk is passed under a series of ultraviolet lights to fortify it with Vitamin D. Finally, the milk is piped into pre-sterilized cans that are vacuum-sealed.

Boost Your Performance

Work through the following strategies and solutions, keeping in mind any question types that proved difficult for you. Then repeat the tricky question types, changing any of your original answers that seem wrong. Check your answers. Keep practising troublesome question types.

Reading and Time Management Strategies

1. Skim and scan instead of reading word by word

Realistically, you do not have the time to read the three passages of text in full. If you try to read every single word in your question paper, you will run out of time before answering all the questions.

The trick is to **read only the important parts**, and that is achieved by **skimming and scanning**. **'Skimming' means reading fast to get the general idea, and 'scanning' means looking for particular information**. Your eyes should be skimming the paragraphs to get the general idea of each, and scanning the paper like radar, looking for keywords, main points and other important information. It is a good idea to circle or underline names, dates and keywords.

How and when to skim

Most students of IELTS-Blog.com reported better results when they skimmed the text first, by reading the title/heading, looking at visuals (if any) and reading the first sentence of every paragraph. Normally this is enough to gain overall understanding of the text.

Then it's time to read the questions, but just the first group. Questions are broken down into groups, with usually questions of one type per group. Read the instructions closely, and the example, for every group of questions before you begin scanning the text.

How and when to scan

Scanning works best when you know what the question is, have seen an example, and thus have an idea about what you're looking for, and what the answer should look like.

Some questions will require you to scan the text to find the answer; others will require reading in detail.

Scanning works best for the following question types:

⇒ **Sentence/Notes/Table/Flow chart/Summary completion**
⇒ **Short-answer questions**
⇒ **Labelling a diagram**
⇒ **Matching features (finding Information in paragraphs)**

Why? Because these question types can be answered by finding a keyword in the paragraph and reading around it, and scanning is the way to find a keyword in text quickly.

Always try to guess what information is missing before you start scanning—this will make finding the answer easier.

2. Be aware of answers that are in sequence

Answers to some types of questions appear sequentially in text. This means that the answer to question 2 appears after the answer to question 1, and the answer to question 3 appears after the answer to question 2. In other words, you won't have to go back in the text to find the next answer if you do the questions sequentially—you will always be moving forward.

This is important because with each answered question you have less and less text to search—which enables you to find the later answers in a group more quickly.

Here are the **question types with answers that follow the order of the text:**

⇒ **Sentence completion (with or without a list of options)**
⇒ **Short-answer questions,**
⇒ **True/False/Not Given,**
⇒ **Yes/No/Not Given,**
⇒ **Multiple choice.**

When solving these types of questions, mark the sentence where you found the answer. To find the next answer, you will only need to search *after* that mark.

Note: When you move on to a question group with a different question type, you may need to go right back to the beginning of the text in search of answers.

3. Use words from the text

Answers to some question types can be copied straight from the text, exactly as they are. This helps you a great deal - firstly, you don't need to think of an answer yourself; secondly, when you copy words accurately you don't have to worry about spelling.

The question types that require words to be copied directly from the text are:

⇒ **Sentence completion (without a list of options)**
⇒ **Short-answer questions**
⇒ **Summary completion (without a list of options)**
⇒ **Table/notes/flowchart completion**
⇒ **Diagram labelling**

4. Read in detail only if you have to

A study that we conducted of IELTS-Blog visitors, helped us to identify these **question types that require reading in detail to find the correct answer:**

⇒ **True/False/Not Given**
⇒ **Yes/No/Not Given**
⇒ **Matching Paragraph Headings**
⇒ **Matching Information**
⇒ **Summary completion with a list of options**
⇒ **Multiple choice questions**

5. Pay close attention to task instructions in the test paper

In IELTS, following instructions is critical - they define the exact way you should answer.

In particular**, the word limit in an answer is crucial**, so when the instructions ask you to answer 'USING NO MORE THAN THREE WORDS AND/OR A NUMBER', only write one, two or three words, and/or a number, but not more. Don't repeat words unnecessarily (for example, if they are already in the sentence that you're required to complete), and don't write two answers/options if they ask for just one.

Note: articles (a/an/the) and prepositions (e.g. in/on/by) count as words.

6. Know when to move on

IELTS is not a 100% kind of test. In years of working with test-takers through IELTS- blog.com, we know of only a very few people who have answered 100% of the reading questions correctly.

Some questions are just harder than others and require more time to answer. This is why there's no shame in putting a question mark next to any tough question and moving on to the next one—it's much better than getting stuck and losing precious time.

If you have time left after all the other questions are answered, go back to the tough questions and try to answer them. Or, if you're nearly out of time—just answer with your best guess.

7. Manage your time

A situation with almost no time left, but still many unanswered questions can be very stressful. With proper preparation you can avoid this in the actual exam.

Spending too long on one passage may lead to the possible loss of all points for a later text and its questions. To prevent this, practise answering the questions for each passage within firm time limits.

How to set up time limits for the three IELTS Academic Reading texts

The three texts in the Academic Reading test are of different lengths ad difficulty. Look at all three texts and choose the one that looks easiest for you. Start with that text and allow about 15 minutes for answering its questions. Move on next to the one that looks the next easiest, allowing 20 minutes for its questions. Reserve the last 25 minutes for answering the most difficult-looking text.

Before you begin reading, write when each time allocation begins and ends. When each time is up, move on to the next text. In IELTS on Paper, make sure you transfer the answers to the Answer Sheet within the time limit you allowed to each particular text. Don't transfer all 40 answers at the very end, do it after finishing each text.

If you have weaker reading skills and find it too difficult, even after practice, to complete the two easiest texts in 15 and 20 minutes try this. Concentrate on the first two easier texts and do them more thoroughly, at the expense of the third, hardest text. Yes, you may not have enough time to finish all the questions in the third text, but spending more time on the first two texts can help you get more correct answers there. Experiment with these different strategies to find which one gives you a larger number of correct answers.

Strategies for Dealing with SPECIFIC Question Types

True/False/Not Given and Yes/No/Not Given

This type of task is problematic because it tests both your English, and logical thinking.

With practice your logical thinking will improve and this type of question will become easier.

When the statement clearly says the same thing as the text, the answer is True, if the statement says the opposite from the text, the answer is False, and if the statement says something that the text doesn't say, it's Not Given. Yes/No/Not Given type works in a very similar way.

To answer this type of question correctly you need to be aware of synonyms as usually the question statement rephrases information stated in the text.

When you practise at home, here is a very powerful way to turn your weaknesses into a strength.

Once you've checked your own answers with those in your book/sample test, and you know which of your answers are wrong, go back are and try to understand exactly why your answers are wrong, and why the ones in the book are correct. This is a very important step in helping you to understand the logic of this question type. Then recall why you answered the way you did, and what *confused* you, what *tricked* you into giving the wrong answer. Try not to make the same mistake the next time.

Matching Paragraph Headings

Proceed paragraph by paragraph in the text

Students often match headings using an over-complicated method. Here is the easy way:

When you match headings, go in the order of paragraphs - not in the order of headings! Go to paragraph 1, look for a suitable heading in the list, then go to paragraph 2, look for a suitable heading, and so on.

In each paragraph, read the first sentence, and then look for a heading. If you can't find the right heading, read the second sentence, then search the list of headings again. If you still can't find the heading, read the last sentence, and then look for a heading. If still you get nothing, then read the whole paragraph before you look for a heading.

This method is based on the fact that **the first sentence of a paragraph often contains its main point.** In many cases reading the first sentence will be enough to find the right heading, but even if you need to read another sentence, this method will still save you time because it doesn't require you to read every paragraph in full. By contrast, students often match headings by going in the order of headings, reading each heading and then trying to find a paragraph to match it—our way saves you from reading the same paragraph over and over.

The task instructions will tell you that a heading can only be used once. In that case, any heading that you matched should be clearly marked as 'taken' on the list (simply by putting a tick '√' next to it). This will save you from considering it again for another paragraph.

Skip tricky paragraphs, come back to them later

If you find a tricky paragraph which is taking up too much time, move on and choose headings for the remaining paragraphs. Then, with fewer headings left, it should be easier to go back and choose one for the tricky paragraph. Even if you end up guessing, your chances of success are greater than before.

Solving Problems During the Reading Test

While preparing for the Reading test, you may still have doubts about how to answer certain types of questions. Don't worry, this is normal. By dealing with issues early on in your preparation, they will affect you much less in the real test! Here are some common problems, with solutions to them.

Problem 1: I am not familiar with the text topic

Problem 2: I am a slow reader

Problem 3: I'm almost out of time, and I still haven't answered all the questions

Problem 4: My spelling is not very good

Problem 5: I have poor handwriting

Problem 6: I am unsure of an answer

 *Scan the QR code to download the **solutions for these problems** from the Treasure Chest or visit https://ielts-blog.com/treasure-chest*

READING CHECKPOINT TEST

IELTS Reading Section

Get Ready for the Checkpoint Test

You should by now have a better idea of yourself as a Reading test performer, as well as of the types of task you may need to do in your actual IELTS test and some helpful strategies to boost your score.

Feeling confident?

If you feel confident, move straight on to the IELTS Reading Checkpoint test on the next page. Before you start, think about your profile - your strengths and weaknesses when taking this type of test.

 *Scan the QR code to access a **blank answer sheet** in the Treasure Chest or visit https://ielts-blog.com/treasure-chest*

Feeling less confident?

If you are still struggling to master all the many aspects of the IELTS Reading test, your best strategy is to go back and repeat the Entry test again.

Doing the Entry test again has several advantages:

- You will be familiar with the texts and can focus on your answers more easily

- You will be more relaxed and will understand better how not to panic

- You will remember some of your previous answers and know how to correct them and why they were wrong.

After repeating the entry test, score yourself again. Was your score higher? Even if it is, review your weaknesses again, and then move on to the Checkpoint test.

IELTS READING CHECKPOINT TEST

READING PASSAGE 1

*You should spend about 20 minutes on **Questions 1 – 13**, which are based on Reading Passage 1 below.*

Why are women becoming unhappier?

A The 21st century American woman enjoys the benefit of more, and better domestic appliances, higher incomes, more control over fertility and relationships, and better education. So, it is paradoxical that the improvements in the objective situation of women in the USA and other industrialised countries over the past 40 years have not been accompanied by perceptions of increased happiness. In fact, women seem to perceive themselves to be both less happy than they were in the 70s and less happy now than men.

B Stephenson and Wolfer's review of the sociological data indicates that, historically, women reported higher levels of subjective well-being than men. By the twenty-first century, women reported happiness levels on a par with, or perhaps lower than those reported by men. Compounding this trend among adults, the US Monitoring the Future study, which since 1976 has been surveying approximately 15,000 US twelfth graders each year about their attitudes, has found that young men have raised levels of happiness, while young women have become slightly less happy.

C Sociologists seem to be unsure about the reasons. Data are inconclusive in terms of whether women now work more hours than men as a result of social changes. However, Hochschild and Machung's work hints at the possibility that women still carry the emotional responsibility in the home and that this is now more challenging for them. Increased divorce rates and growing numbers of children born out of wedlock may have added to women's emotional burdens. Yet, research data tend to suggest that levels of happiness are not significantly different between those women with, and those without children. Other sociologists like Kimball and Willis suggest that the hopefulness and idealism that accompanied the growth of the women's movement in the 70's have gradually weakened. Perhaps connected to this, the largest decline in happiness among women was among the group that had attended university, though this reflects the steadily increasing proportion of women who have been attending college across the past 40 years. In fact, irrespective of the age, marital, labour market, or fertility status of the group analysed, data suggest that both the absolute decline in happiness among women in the United States, and the even larger decline relative to men, seems to be widespread. In Europe, trends are similar with perhaps an even greater decline in the happiness of women relative to men. The attempt to find a critical, explanatory variable has so far proven elusive, however.

D   With which aspects of their lives are women now less satisfied? A number of survey questions have explored satisfaction across a number of domains: work, financial situation, family, health, and job satisfaction. Women and men remain similarly satisfied with their work when compared with the past. With financial situation perceptions have changed. Women begin the sampling period reporting financial satisfaction that is similar to that for men. However, women's financial satisfaction declines through the 80s and 90s, and, by the end of the sample period, women are substantially less satisfied with their household financial situation than are men. What is more, the magnitude of the decline in women's satisfaction with their financial situation is similar to the decline in women's happiness overall.

E   On average, women are less happy with their marriage than men, and women have become less happy with their marriage over time. However, men have also become less happy with their marriage; thus, the gender gap in marital happiness has been largely stable. Marital happiness is more closely linked to general happiness for women, with the correlation between overall happiness and marital happiness being 0.4 for married men and 0.5 for married women. When asked to rate their health on a four-point scale from poor to excellent, women throughout the period report lower health satisfaction than do men. In contrast, men's subjective health assessment has not changed much over this period.

F   Returning to the teenagers, it seems that the subjective well-being of girls is falling and the well-being of boys rising. There appears to be increasing ambition among young women beyond the domestic sphere, with greater importance attached to being successful and being able to find steady work, or making a contribution to society. These data arguably suggest that women's life satisfaction may have become more complicated as women have increased the number of domains in which they wish to succeed. Moreover, the data point to rising pressures beyond the much-discussed work-family trade-off.

G   One possibility is that broad social shifts such as those brought on by the changing role of women in society fundamentally alter what measures of subjective well-being are actually capturing, leading to falling average satisfaction as it becomes difficult to achieve the same degree of satisfaction in multiple domains. Perhaps the puzzle is less one of finding out why women see themselves as less happy and more one of unravelling why men's life happiness has not declined in line with women's.

Questions 1 – 5

Do the following statements agree with the information given in the text? In boxes **1 – 5** on your answer sheet write:

TRUE if the statement agrees with the information
FALSE if the statement contradicts the information
NOT GIVEN if there is no information on this

1 Higher education correlates negatively with levels of women's happiness.
2 Social research is close to finding the explanation for women's growing unhappiness.
3 Women are still satisfied with their male work colleagues.
4 Satisfaction with health has not changed much for both men and women.
5 Women's rising life ambitions may be making personal wellbeing more difficult.

Questions 6 – 8

Complete the summary below. Write **NO MORE THAN ONE WORD** from the text for each answer.
Write your answers in boxes **6 – 8** on your answer sheet.

Feelings of (**6**) _____ seem to be decreasing for women over the past forty years, despite improvements in their life circumstances. Social scientists remain (**7**) _____ about why this is the case. Men's levels of life satisfaction have not (**8**) _____ to a similar extent, and uncovering explanations for that might help solve this mystery.

Questions 9 – 13

Reading Passage 1 has 7 paragraphs **A – G**. Which paragraph contains the following information?
Write your answers in boxes **9 – 13** on your answer sheet.

9   Early research evidence indicating women felt happier than men.
10 Generally, men and women are less satisfied with their marriages.
11 Women's unhappiness may reflect the emotional drag of home life.
12 International explanations for women's unhappiness are hard to uncover.
13 Changes in women's roles cloud what happiness studies can reveal.

READING PASSAGE 2

*You should spend about 20 minutes on **Questions 14 – 27**, which are based on Reading Passage 2 below.*

The changing vocal world of the humpback whale

A   In the dark world of the world's oceans, whales depend on echolocation – the use of sound for navigation. Only 1 per cent of surface light travels to a depth of 100 meters; at 600 meters the sun's illumination equals that of starlight. Lacking an external ear, they detect sound waves via a fat pad between mandible and middle ear. Among the cetaceans, humpback whales are recognized by scientists as one of the most vocally diverse and exciting species. The cetologist, Peter Beamish, tested the navigational skills of humpback whales in the dark. After building a maze in a Newfoundland bay for a humpback rescued from a fishing net, he blindfolded the whale with rubber drain plungers. Before being set free, the humpback managed to find its way through the maze, thereby demonstrating the effectiveness of echolocation.

B   In 1967, the biologist Roger Payne started making and analysing recordings of the sounds of humpbacks off Bermuda. Working from hundreds of hours of tape recordings taken on the breeding ground, Payne contended that the sounds they heard were more than idle chatter. They described the sounds as notes uttered in succession which together formed a recognizable sequence or pattern in time. In other words, they were songs with distinctive themes. All the whales in a breeding group appeared to sing the same songs, over and over again.

C   Scientists have been studying humpback whale songs for nearly fifty years, but there are strange things about them which resist explanation. For instance, only the male whales sing these amazing songs, so it is generally assumed that the song is to attract the attention of females. However, no one has ever seen a female whale approach a singing male. Instead, other males seem to be more interested. When they approach the singer, he stops singing, and the two males go off silently together for a little while, and then they separate.

D   In any year, whales sing identical songs in Hawaii and Mexico, breeding areas that are 4,500 kilometres apart. How is this possible? Perhaps they hear the songs across long distances or learn them during the summer months, when different groups gather in the north to feed. More remarkable than the geographic consistency is the change in calls over time. Slight variations in the songs occur each year. But, as with evolution, these changes can make huge leaps in a short time. Variation in whale songs is evidence that cetaceans have culture, which can change over time and vary across oceans. The Australian biologist, Mike Noad, and colleagues, found evidence of a 'cultural revolution' in the Southern Hemisphere. In 1996 two male humpbacks from the Indian Ocean arrived in the Pacific with a new song. Within two years, all the Pacific males had changed their tune, picking up the migrants' songs. An explanation of this switch is not so straightforward. A preference for novelty is one possibility, though this theory seems to be contradicted by the observation that all whales in a particular area sing the same song in a given year. Although the cause of this dramatic change is still unclear, the knowledge that cetacean cultures endure and change over time, and that culture is not the unique domain of humans is likely to radically transform perception of these mammals.

E Unfortunately, whales, and an understanding of their calls, are under a new threat. Noise that degrades information exchange comes in many forms, and it may change the use of a communication system and possibly derail communication all together. Dependency on sound makes whales vulnerable to the rising level of noise in the oceans. The number of cargo ships has tripled in the past 75 years, with larger vessels plying the seas each year. These human-generated, chronic sounds are akin to a smog of acoustic noise. Fishermen employing depth finders and acoustical gear in their search for fish add to this noise. The constant underwater din, which can impact whales' ability to hunt and reproduce, is punctuated by intense pulses from seismic air guns, used to plot oil and gas deposits along the ocean shelf. Among the loudest sounds produced by humans, these pulses reach across entire oceans and may be responsible for recent whale strandings.

F Naval exercises using high-decibel mid-frequency sonar for antisubmarine training can also harm whales. Mass strandings of beaked whales have occurred around the world after military tests. In 2000, 13 beaked whales and two minkes stranded in the Bahamas after the US Navy deployed mid-frequency sonar. Four of the whales had unusual haemorrhages near their ears. In 2002, 14 beaked whales were stranded in the Canary Islands after a test. Ten of them had gas bubbles in their blood vessels, clear evidence of decompression sickness. The whales may have reacted to the ear-splitting noises by heading for the surface too quickly, disoriented by the sonar. Given that symptoms of the bends have never been found in these deep-diving whales, it is also possible that the noises caused the bubbles to form in the bloodstream of vulnerable whales. There is evidence that, in the laboratory, cetaceans attempt to avoid noise and increase breathing rates, a sign of stress. In the acoustic smog of the modern ocean, there may be nowhere for dolphins and whales to go. Noise can also affect communication. Humpback whales change their songs in the presence of active sonar, extending their calls to compensate for the acoustic interference on their breeding grounds. The situation is unlikely to improve in the near future.

Questions 14 – 19

Reading Passage 2 has 6 paragraphs **A – F**. Choose the correct heading for paragraphs **A – F** from the list of headings below.

Write the correct number (**i – viii**) in boxes **14 – 19** on your answer sheet.

i	The mysteries of humpback song
ii	How males attract females
iii	Whale songs as shapers of cultural change
iv	Whales navigate successfully, just by sound
v	Singing the same song in every country
vi	Whale sounds involve song-like patterns
vii	Threats of noise to whale communication systems
viii	Military activities under water and their health impacts

14   Paragraph A
15   Paragraph B
16   Paragraph C
17   Paragraph D
18   Paragraph E
19   Paragraph F

Questions 20 – 23

*Choose the correct letter **A, B, C or D**. Write the correct letter in boxes **20 – 23** on your answer sheet.*

20 What was the key outcome of Peter Beamish's research?

    A   It indicated that whales could build a maze

    B   A blindfolded whale could escape captivity

    C   Sound is crucial to navigation by whales

    D   Whales were able to get through mazes

21 What does the writer say about male and female singing patterns?

    A   Female whales sing to male whales only

    B   Female whales get close to male whales when they hear them sing

    C   Male whales seem to attract other males when they sing

    D   Male whales pair up and go off together to sing before splitting up again

22 Mike Noad's studies found that....

    A   New songs from a different location are immediately adopted by other whales

    B   Whales have their own distinctive culture and it changes

    C   Whale songs change because whales like new forms of communication

    D   The causes of changes in song are becoming clear

23 As a result of underwater military exercises,

    A   Whales' breathing rates speeded up

    B   All of the whales suffered from the bends or bleeding

    C   A few of the whales ended up with hearing problems

    D   Most whales ended up on the beach

IELTS Reading Section

Questions 24 – 27

Complete the summary of paragraphs **A**, **B** and **C** using the words in the box below.

Write your answers in boxes **24 – 27** on your answer sheet.

Whales carry out (**24**) _____ by detecting sound waves. Humpbacks are one of the species with a greater range of sounds. Experiments show that this enables them to negotiate mazes even when (**25**) _____. Humpback 'songs' are not random but represent a patterned (**26**) _____ in succession. The songs are repeated by all whales in a group. Whale song has been studied for a long time but their mysteries (**27**) _____ our ability to explain them fully. Only the males perform these songs.

---

illumination	recognised	blindfolded
themes	approach	wave
resumed	attract	sequence
navigation	resist	
tested	separate	

90 IELTS Test Mastery :: Academic

READING PASSAGE 3

*You should spend about 20 minutes on **Questions 28 – 40**, which are based on Reading Passage 3 below.*

Wave energy – a UK perspective

Waves are generated by the wind as it blows across the ocean surface. They travel great distances and so act as an efficient energy transport mechanism across thousands of kilometres. The energy can be captured by various devices, which produce enough movement either of air or water to drive generators that convert the energy into electricity.

A   The energy contained in ocean waves can potentially provide an unlimited source of renewable energy. Ocean waves are created by the interaction of wind with the surface of the sea and the UK has wave power levels that are amongst the highest in the world. The initial solar power level of about 100W/m2 is concentrated to an average wave power level of 70kW/metre of crest length. This figure rises to an average of 170kW/metre of crest length during the winter, and to more than 1,000kW/metre during storms. Wave energy converters extract and convert this energy into a useful form. The conversion usually makes use of either mechanical motion or fluid pressure, and there are numerous techniques for achieving it. The mechanical energy is then converted to electrical power using a generator. Wave energy converters can be deployed either on the shoreline or in the deeper waters offshore. East-facing sites in the UK are unsuitable because of the limited energy associated with easterly winds, while bottom friction reduces power levels where the water depth is less than 80 metres. As a result, the inshore resource is usually only one-quarter or less of the deep-water resource.

B   The three main types of wave power machines either sit on the shoreline or are free-floating.

Oscillating water column
An oscillating water column is a partially submerged, hollow structure that is installed in the ocean. It is open to the sea below the water line, enclosing a column of air on top of a column of water. Waves cause the water column to rise and fall, which in turn compresses and depresses the air column. This trapped air is allowed to flow to and from the atmosphere via a Wells turbine, which has the ability to rotate in the same direction regardless of the direction of the airflow. The rotation of the turbine generates electricity.

Buoyant moored device

A buoyant moored device floats on or just below the surface of the water and is moored to the sea floor. A wave power machine needs to resist the motion of the waves in order to generate power: part of the machine needs to move while another part remains still. In this type of device, the mooring is static and arranged such that the waves' motion will move only one part of the machine.

Hinged contour device

A hinged contour device is able to operate at greater depths than the buoyant moored device. Here, the resistance to the waves is created by the alternate motion of the waves, which raises and lowers different sections of the machine relative to each other, pushing hydraulic fluid through hydraulic pumps to generate electricity.

The main problem with wave power is that the sea is an unforgiving environment. An economically-viable wave power machine will need to generate power over a wide range of wave sizes, as well as withstand the largest and most severe storms and other potential problems such as algae, barnacles and corrosion.

C   Due to lack of long-term commercial operating experience, actual cost data is virtually non-existent. The estimates always show projected cost per kWh, falling over time due to better designs and increasing unit size. Given the state of technology there is little doubt that many designs can generate electricity but the key question is can they do so cheaply. It would be straightforward to build very strong devices capable of withstanding all the storm conditions expected - the difficulty is constructing at minimum capital cost and having minimum operating cost (for maintenance and repair) so that the overall cost of generation is kept as low as possible and is competitive with alternative forms of generation.

D   There are two wave power devices in the UK. Total installed capacity currently stands at 1.25 megawatts. The first type of device is the LIMPET (Land Installed Marine Powered Energy Transformer), a 500-kilowatt shoreline oscillating water column on the Scottish island of Islay. The second, the 750-kilowatt Pelamis sea snake, is an example of a hinged contour device. It is the first deep-water grid-connected trial and is currently installed at the European Marine Energy Centre in Scotland, where it has been undergoing testing.

E   Marine energy could provide around 20 per cent of the UK's electricity needs but only if there is sufficient investment in the appropriate technology. In the short-term the initial set-up costs of marine energy are high as it requires extensive research and development. Yet it is clear that sufficient investment now could lead to a strong UK marine energy sector. The UK is in prime position to accelerate commercial progress in the marine energy sector and secure economic value by selling marine energy devices, developing wave and tidal stream farms and creating new revenues from electricity generation.

F   Wind-generated waves on the ocean surface have a total estimated power of 90 million gigawatts worldwide. Due to the direction of the prevailing winds and the size of the Atlantic Ocean, the UK has wave power levels that are among the highest in the world. Wave energy has the potential to provide as much renewable energy as the wind industry.

Questions 28 – 32

Do the following statements agree with the views of the writer of the text?

In boxes **28 – 32** on your answer sheet write:

> **YES** if the statement agrees with the writer's views
> **NO** if the statement doesn't agree with the writer's views
> **NOT GIVEN** if it is impossible to say what the writer thinks about this

28 The conversion of wave energy is restricted to deep water installations

29 To be cost effective wave generators must be able to operate across waves of varying dimension

30 The current technology is well advanced in terms of cheap generation of wave energy

31 Existing wave power devices are located right across the UK

32 The UK is poised to be a key player in marine energy if sufficient investment is undertaken.

Questions 33 – 36

According to the text, to which device (**A, B or C**) does each statement apply?

Write the correct letter in boxes **33 – 36** on your answer sheet.

> **A** Oscillating water column
> **B** Buoyant moored device
> **C** Hinged contour device

33 This device is a combination of an immovable part and another section which engages with wave action.

34 This device uses differential wave action to move its parts up and down in response to variable wave strength.

35 The turning movement of the generating engine in this device produces electrical power.

36 This device uses fluid mechanics to harvest and convert wave energy.

Questions 37 – 40

*Passage 3 has 6 sections **A – F**. Which section contains the following information?*

*Write your answers in boxes **37 – 40** on your answer sheet.*

37 The impact of geographical location and water depth on output of energy

38 The absence of comparative analysis of construction and running costs

39 The importance of putting money into wave technology to build a strong commercial market

40 The difficulties caused by meteorological conditions and marine life forms

 The answers are located in the IELTS Answers section at the end of this book.

Finished the Checkpoint test?

When you have added up your score on the Checkpoint test, repeat the review process to build awareness of your ongoing weaknesses, and to chart where your test techniques and understanding have improved. Repeat the checkpoint test a few days later.

At the end of this book there will be a final test for you to try (**Exit test**) but this time you should take all four parts of the IELTS test at the same sitting (Listening, Reading, Writing and Speaking), and then award scores for all parts of the Exit test.

Now, it's time to move on to the Writing section on the next page.

WRITING ENTRY TEST

Get Ready for IELTS Writing Tasks 1 and 2

In the IELTS Writing test you will be asked to write in response to two tasks - Task 1 and Task 2. The Writing test takes **60 minutes - 20 minutes for Task 1 and 40 minutes for Task 2.** You are expected to write a minimum of **150 words in response to Task 1 and 250 words in response to Task 2.** You may lose marks if you don't write enough words. **You can respond to the tasks in any order** (Task 1 then Task 2, or Task 2 then Task 1).

Writing Task 1

Task 1 involves describing information that is provided. **It is worth only 1/3 (one third) of your Overall Writing Score.**

Reading through Task 1 carefully is important, as is planning how to structure your written response. We recommend spending a few minutes reading the task and looking carefully at the chart, graph, map or diagram to identify relevant, key data, while at the same time planning how to organise the content of your paragraphs, and thinking of appropriate vocabulary.

To respond well to a Task 1 topic:

- Highlight key trends and features from the visual in your response
- Write about similarities and differences between two sets of data where appropriate
- Structure your response with clear introduction, overview and body paragraphs
- Use linking words and phrases for a smooth flow between sentences / paragraphs
- Use accurate grammar and spelling, as well as appropriate, formal vocabulary

Writing Task 2

Task 2 involves discussing/offering your views on a given topic. It is worth 2/3 (two thirds) of your Overall Writing Score.

There are **4 different question types in IELTS Writing Task 2**. Being familiar with the demands of each type is important.

It is vital to read each Task carefully and plan the structure of your response. We recommend not just reading the task but thinking carefully about what type of task it is. This will shape how best to structure your opinions and knowledge of the social issue involved.

To respond well to a Task 2 topic:

- Develop your point of view clearly
- Write in clear paragraphs, each with a clear, central idea
- Make your writing easy to read, with few words/sentences crossed out
- Include relevant ideas, and avoid being repetitive
- Write accurately and with a variety of grammar and linking words
- Use a good range of appropriate, and formal vocabulary
- Avoid copying/repeating too many expressions used in the task wording.

General guidelines for answering Writing questions

We recommend you **write down a plan for each writing task and refer to it as you write your paragraphs.**

You need to follow the rules of capitalisation in your written responses, in order to receive full marks for Grammatical Range and Accuracy. Don't write your entire response in UPPERCASE or lowercase letters.

To prevent your task response looking unplanned and messy, avoid crossing out words or phrases too often.

Appropriate vocabulary, correct grammar and spelling, are important. Focus on what the task requires, with writing that flows and connects well from sentence to sentence.

 *Scan the QR code to access a **blank answer sheet** in the Treasure Chest or visit https://ielts-blog.com/treasure-chest*

Are you ready? Start the Entry Test now.

IELTS Writing Section

IELTS WRITING ENTRY TEST

TASK 1

You should spend about 20 minutes on this task.

The chart below shows the amount of tea and coffee imported by Canada, UK, USA and Italy in 2015 in tonnes.

Summarise the information by selecting and reporting the key features, and make any relevant comparisons.

Write at least 150 words.

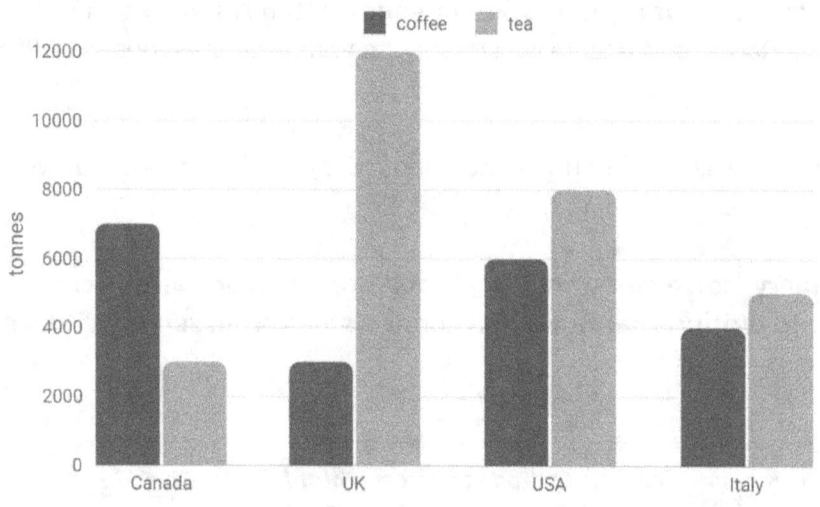

Coffee and tea imported by Canada, UK, USA and Italy, 2015

TASK 2

You should spend about 40 minutes on this task.

Write about the following topic:

> **People should continue to work beyond traditional retirement age. Do you agree or disagree?**
>
> **Give reasons for your answer and include any relevant ideas from your own knowledge or experience.**

Write at least 250 words.

Score, Review then Practise

Score your Entry Test

 Now you have finished the Entry Test, compare your written responses with the samples in the IELTS Writing Answers at the end of this book.

The sample responses would probably receive a **Band score of 9 in IELTS**.

Now try to **give yourself a score** for your own writing using the tables below to guide your assessment of your performance on each of the four criteria. Remember, the IELTS band scale goes from 0 - 9.

Don't worry if you give yourself scores that are too high or too low, the aim is to build your awareness both of how scores are awarded, and how different your written performances were from those with a very high score.

Add the four individual scores together and divide your total score by 4 for an approximate overall band score for each Task.

Writing Task 1

Assessment Criteria	What it means	Your score (0-9)
Task Achievement (TA)	A high score means you selected and described all the **important features** of the task in your writing, identified main trends or differences and quoted data accurately.	
Coherence and Cohesion (CC)	A high score means your **paragraphs were arranged logically,** and your selected **information flowed** from sentence to sentence **via appropriate connecting words/expressions**.	
Lexical Resource (LR)	A high score means you used **appropriate, varied and extensive vocabulary.**	
Grammatical Range and Accuracy (GRA)	A high score means you used **different sentence types with accuracy and flexibility.**	
Total Task 1 Score	(TA + CC + LR + GRA) / 4	

Writing Task 2

Assessment Criteria	What it means	Your score (0-9)
Task Response (TR)	A high score means you have covered **all parts of the task** in your response, expressing **relevant ideas** and fully **developing** and **supporting** them in your writing.	
Coherence and Cohesion (CC)	A high score means your **ideas were arranged logically in paragraphs,** and your **information flowed** from sentence to sentence **via appropriate connecting words/expressions**.	
Lexical Resource (LR)	A high score means you used **appropriate, varied and extensive vocabulary** and **topic-specific** phrases naturally.	
Grammatical Range and Accuracy (GRA)	A high score means you used **different sentence types with accuracy and flexibility.**	
Total Task 2 Score	(TR + CC + LR + GRA) / 4	

Now calculate your total writing score using this formula:

Writing Task 1 Score x 1/3 + Writing Task 2 Score x 2/3 = Total Writing Score.

Review

After scoring your writing on all four criteria for both tasks, review each task in detail, focusing on one criterion at a time. Identify weaknesses in your language and writing. Compare with Band 9 sample responses. Here are a few questions to guide you:

- Did you use the time well - about 20 minutes for Task 1 and 40 minutes for Task 2?
- Did you do what the question in Task 1 and Task 2 asked?
- Was your grammar accurate - verb tenses, verb agreement, pronouns, for example?
- Did you use good linking words within and between sentences?
- Did you use paragraphing successfully?
- Did you use a good variety of appropriate vocabulary, correctly spelled?
- Were your responses relevant and not repetitive?

Practise

After identifying your writing strengths and weaknesses, move on to the next section and practise all IELTS Writing task types and language features, focusing on challenging areas.

Boost Your Performance

For tricky writing activities, review the test strategies (pages 123, 153) and check solutions to common writing issues. Then retry the same two tasks, changing the parts of your writing that seem weak.

WRITING TASK 1 PRACTICE

WHAT'S INSIDE:

- **Practise the Question Types**
- **Boost Your Performance**

IELTS Writing Task 1 Section

Practise the IELTS Writing Task 1 Types

| QUESTION TYPE 1 | Map

Tasks involving maps of indoor or outdoor areas often ask you to compare the same area or facility by describing the changes from one date to another.

The best strategy is to make sure your response exactly mirrors what the task asks you to do, by reading the task instructions carefully, and noting key changes across the different times.

It is also helpful to use compass directions North/East/South/West to locate specific changes shown on the map across the two dates.

An introduction, overview, and clear body paragraphs are also important.

Study this Task 1 Map question and complete Activities 1-16 that follow.

> The plans below show the layout of the ground floor of a school library in 2001, and how it changed as a result of renovations in 2009.
>
> Summarise the information by selecting and reporting the main features, and make comparisons where relevant.
>
> Write at least 150 words

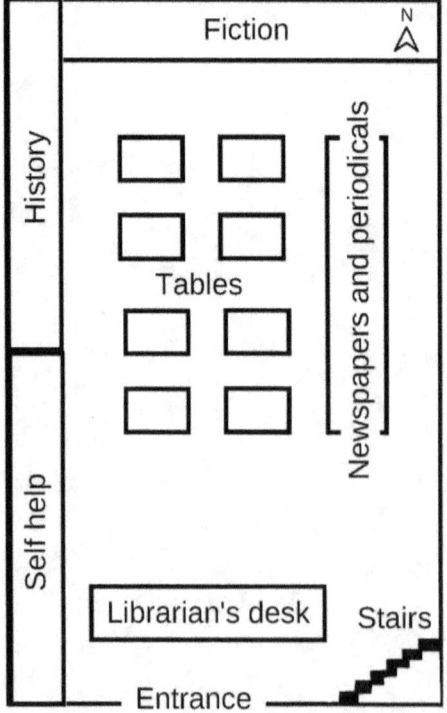

Library ground floor 2001

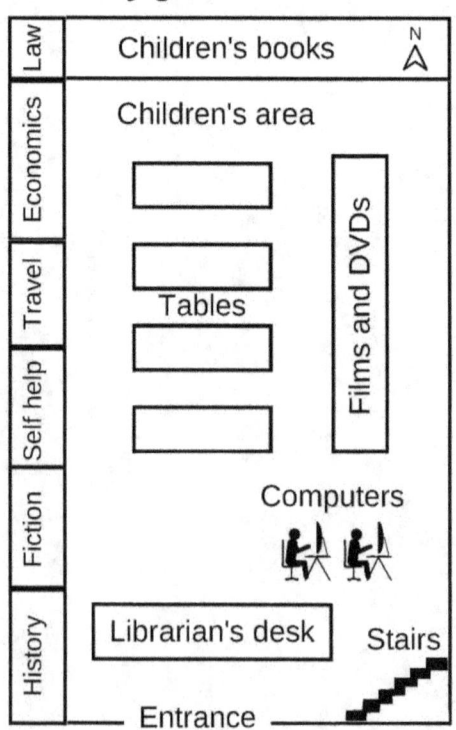

Library ground floor 2009

IELTS Writing Task 1 Section

Activities 1 - 4   Get started and build the INTRODUCTION

The answers to all Activities are located in the IELTS Answers section at the end of this book.

1   How many paragraphs seem better suited for a good response?

   a) 3
   b) 4
   c) 5

2   What is the function of the first paragraph (the Introduction)?

   a) Introduce the task.
   b) Introduce the task and say how many paragraphs the response will have.
   c) Introduce the task and give an overview of what the maps show.

3   What should you do in the first paragraph?

   a) copy the words exactly from the task
   b) change as many words as you can
   c) change all the words in the task

4   The verb tense for the first sentence should be:

   a) The maps showed
   b) The maps are showing
   c) The maps show

Activities 5 - 6   Build the OVERVIEW

5   What is the function of the second paragraph (The Overview)?

   a) To summarise the most important changes
   b) To express an opinion about why the changes happened
   c) To predict what will happen in the future

6   A suitable length for the Overview should be approximately:

   a) 5-6 sentences
   b) 3-4 sentences
   c) 1-2 sentences

IELTS Writing Task 1 Section

Activities 7 - 8 The language for the INTRODUCTION and OVERVIEW

7 Use the words in the box to complete this Introduction and Overview:

| were | show | modernised | overall |

Introduction

The two maps _____ the changes that occurred to the ground floor of a library over a period of eight years, from 2001 to 2009.

Overview

_____, what can clearly be seen is that the library was _____ with the addition of a film and DVD section as well as a dedicated area for computers. In addition, several, new sections _____ added to the ground floor.

8 Complete this summary about the Introduction and Overview (one word for each space):

The Introduction presents the writing _____ using somewhat different words. The overview includes a _____ of the main changes on the map. The first sentence uses the _____ tense and the other sentences use the _____ tense because they describe past events (2001-2009).

Activities 9 - 11 Build BODY PARAGRAPH 1
(Describing the library in 2001)

9 Tick (√) any ideas below that seem a good strategy for Body Paragraph 1:

a) It is a good idea to talk about the map using the logic of directions like north, south, east, and west.
b) It seems helpful to focus on the more important features.
c) It is important to describe everything.
d) It is important to write about 90 words.
e) It is important to try to avoid being too repetitive and mechanical.

IELTS Writing Task 1 Section

10 Study the maps. Put 'northern', 'eastern', 'western' into this paragraph:

Body Paragraph 1

In 2001 the _____ side of the library contained just two categories of books, self help and history. The fiction area was located along the _____ wall of the library. The centre of the ground floor used to house eight, single tables. The space along the _____ wall on the ground floor was occupied by the newspaper and periodical section. The librarian's desk was located next to the library's entrance and to its right there was a stairway leading to the first floor.

11 The main function of Body Paragraph 1 is to describe:

a) one or two features of the library in 2001 systematically.
b) all features of the library in 2001 clearly and systematically.
c) the key features of the library in 2001 clearly and systematically.

Activities 12 - 15   Build BODY PARAGRAPH 2
               (Describing changes to the library by 2009)

12 Choose the correct sentence to start the paragraph:

a) By 2009, several modification have taken place.
b) By 2009, several modifications had taken place.
c) In 2009, several modifications had taken place.
d) By 2009, several modifications took place.

13 Put the missing prepositions from the box into the paragraph:

| to | by | with | along | for | in |

Body Paragraph 2

_____ 2009, several modifications had taken place. A few more book categories had been introduced _____ the western wall, including fiction, travel, law and economics. The old fiction area had been turned into a children's book section, _____ a separate area having been created especially for children. The single tables _____ the centre had been replaced with four, longer tables, allowing more seating _____ library patrons. The newspaper and periodical section had been replaced with a film and DVD section, and close _____ the entrance and stairs, two new, computer stations had been added. The library's entrance and the adjacent area, including the librarian's desk and stairway had remained unchanged.

IELTS Writing Task 1 Section

14 Which words in Body Paragraph 2 could these replace appropriately?

changes   could replace _____
added   ⇒   _____
dedicated   ⇒   _____
chairs   ⇒   _____
customers   ⇒   _____

15 **Choice of tense:**

Because the year being discussed is 2009, and because the changes had happened in the period between 2001 and 2009, and thus not necessarily all in 2009, the tense used most often in Body Paragraph 2 is the...

a) simple past
b) present perfect
c) past perfect

Activity 16   Write a complete report

16 Now write your own report. Spend no more than 20 minutes and write at least 150 words.

_____

_____

When you have finished, compare your report to the sample report we have provided in the Treasure Chest.

 *Scan the QR code to access **sample responses for all the activities** in the Treasure Chest or visit https://ielts-blog.com/treasure-chest*

QUESTION TYPE 2   Process Diagram

Tasks involving process diagrams have a clear progression as they usually go from a beginning to an end in a series of a steps.

The best strategy is to study the diagram closely, identify the steps, decide how best to divide up the process being shown, and think of the kind of core language that will be needed (e.g. First/Then/After that/Next/Finally) and the use of passive forms (e.g. 'is accepted/rejected')

It's also a good idea to try to think of possible synonyms for words on the diagram, and not just always copy words provided. An Introduction and short overview are also important.

Study this Task 1 Process Diagram question and complete Activities 1-9 that follow.

> **The diagram below shows the stages in buying a house.**
>
> **Summarise the information by selecting and reporting the main features, and make comparisons where relevant.**
>
> **Write at least 150 words**

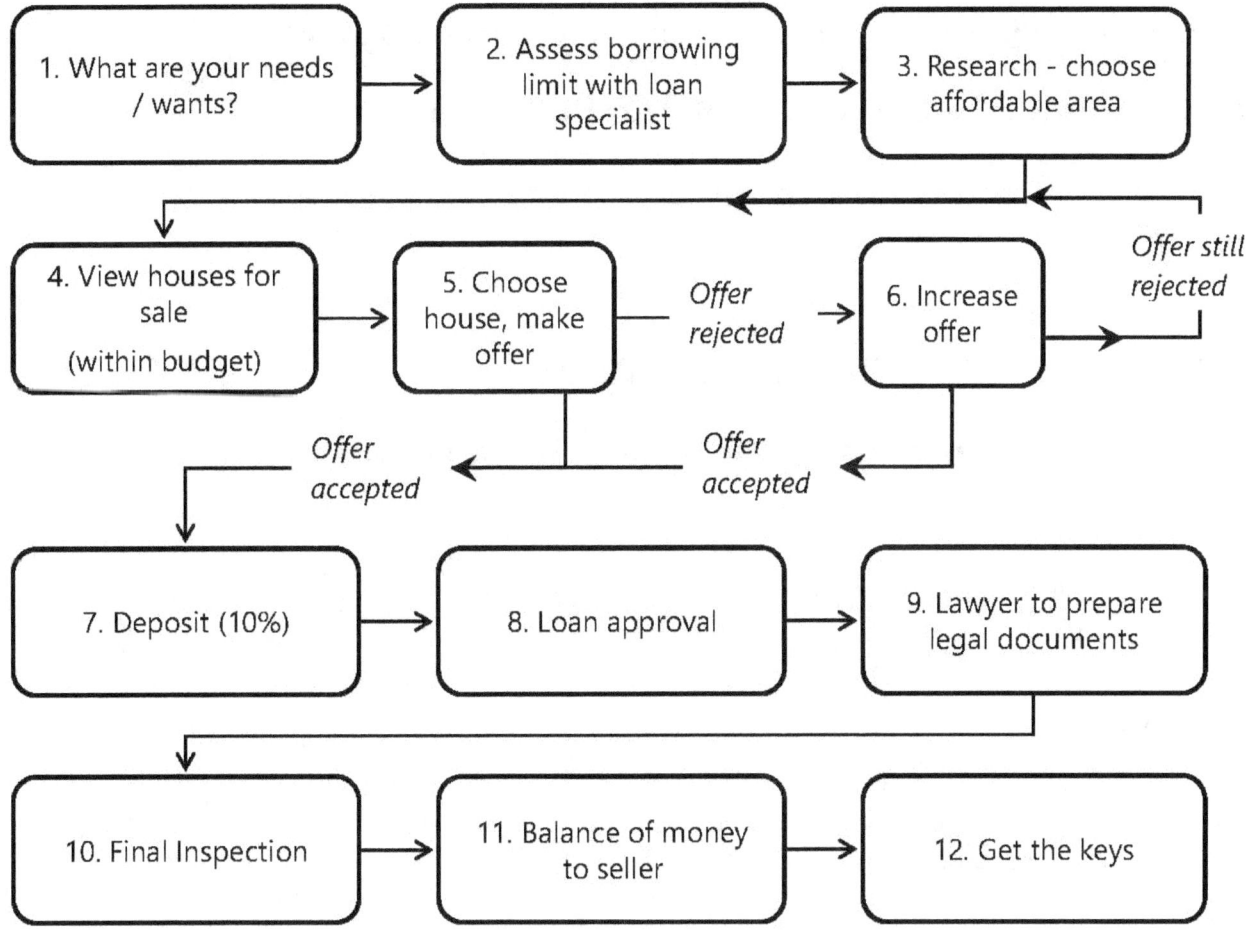

IELTS Writing Task 1 Section

Activities 1 - 4   Get started and build the INTRODUCTION

The answers to all Activities are located in the IELTS Answers section at the end of this book.

1   Look at the diagram. Which tense should be used in the Introduction?

   a) present simple (e.g. 'It shows')
   b) present continuous (e.g. 'It is showing')
   c) present perfect (e.g. 'It has shown')

2   Choose two verbs from the box which best complete the Introduction:

tells	shows	demonstrates	outlined	covers

   Introduction

   The diagram _____ the main step in buy a house. It _____ financial and legal issues, view and making offers.

3   Correct the three grammatical errors in the Introduction in Activity 2.

4   Which words in the Introduction (Activity 2) could these replace?

   'stages'   could replace   _____
   'purchasing'   ⇒   _____
   'aspects'   ⇒   _____

Activity 5   Build the OVERVIEW

5   A short overview comes next. Put the steps below in the correct order:

   Overview

   Overall, there are three principal parts to the process: _____ , _____ , and finally, _____ .

   Steps

   - making financial arrangements
   - finding the right house
   - negotiating a price

Activities 6 - 8   Build the BODY PARAGRAPHS

6 A process involves steps, one following another. Put these 'time sequence' words correctly into the Body Paragraphs:

| Once | Then | As soon as | After | After that | The first step | Once |

Body Paragraph 1

_____involves establishing your housing needs and then calculating a borrowing ceiling with the help of a loan expert. _____, a prospective purchaser needs to look for affordable areas in their town or city, and go to look at suitable houses, within budget.

Body Paragraph 2

_____a house has been chosen an offer is made. If it is rejected, the buyer can either propose an increased price or choose another house and make a new offer on that one. This step repeats until the buyer's offer has been accepted.

Body Paragraph 3

_____ the price has been agreed, a deposit of 10% needs to be paid to the vendor. _____the purchaser's loan has been approved by the bank, a lawyer is required to prepare the legal documents of transfer. _____a final inspection of the house is carried out and the balance of the selling price is paid to the seller. _____that money is cleared, the new owner receives the keys.

7 Passives help build process descriptions. Find <u>two</u> examples each for the <u>present passive</u>, and the <u>present perfect passive</u> in the Body Paragraphs.

Present passive
Example 1 _____   Example 2 _____

Present perfect passive
Example 1 _____   Example 2 _____

IELTS Writing Task 1 Section

8   In Activity 6, not using 'you' or 'we' makes the writing more formal. Use the passive to rewrite these 3 sentences:

Example: First, <u>you establish</u> your housing needs -> *First, housing needs <u>are established</u>*.

1) Then you look for affordable areas.   _____
2) Next, you choose a house and make an offer. _____
3) If it is accepted, you pay a 10% deposit.   _____

Activity 9   Write a complete report

9   Now write your own report. Spend no more than 20 minutes and write at least 150 words.

_____

_____

When you have finished, compare your report to the sample report we have provided in the Treasure Chest.

 *Scan the QR code to access **sample responses** for all the activities in the Treasure Chest or visit https://ielts-blog.com/treasure-chest*

QUESTION TYPE 3   Graph

Writing about graphs can be challenging as there is a lot of detail, and you have to focus on the information carefully in order not to get mixed up. It is important to be clear about the horizontal axis and vertical axis and what they are describing.

The best strategy is to circle the key features on the graph so that you can locate them quickly, and to remember the kind of language for describing graphs (e.g. rose, increased, decreased significantly/ slightly/marginally, remained steady).

It is also important to decide how to divide up your answer into clear paragraphs, each with its own function. An introduction and short overview are also important.

Study this Task 1 Graph question and complete Activities 1-9 that follow.

Task Question

The graph shows the percentage occupancy of caravan parks and hotel rooms between June '08 and September '09.

Summarise the information by selecting and reporting the key features, and make any relevant comparisons.

Write at least 150 words.

Percentage occupancy rates in caravan parks and hotels Jun '08 - Sep '09

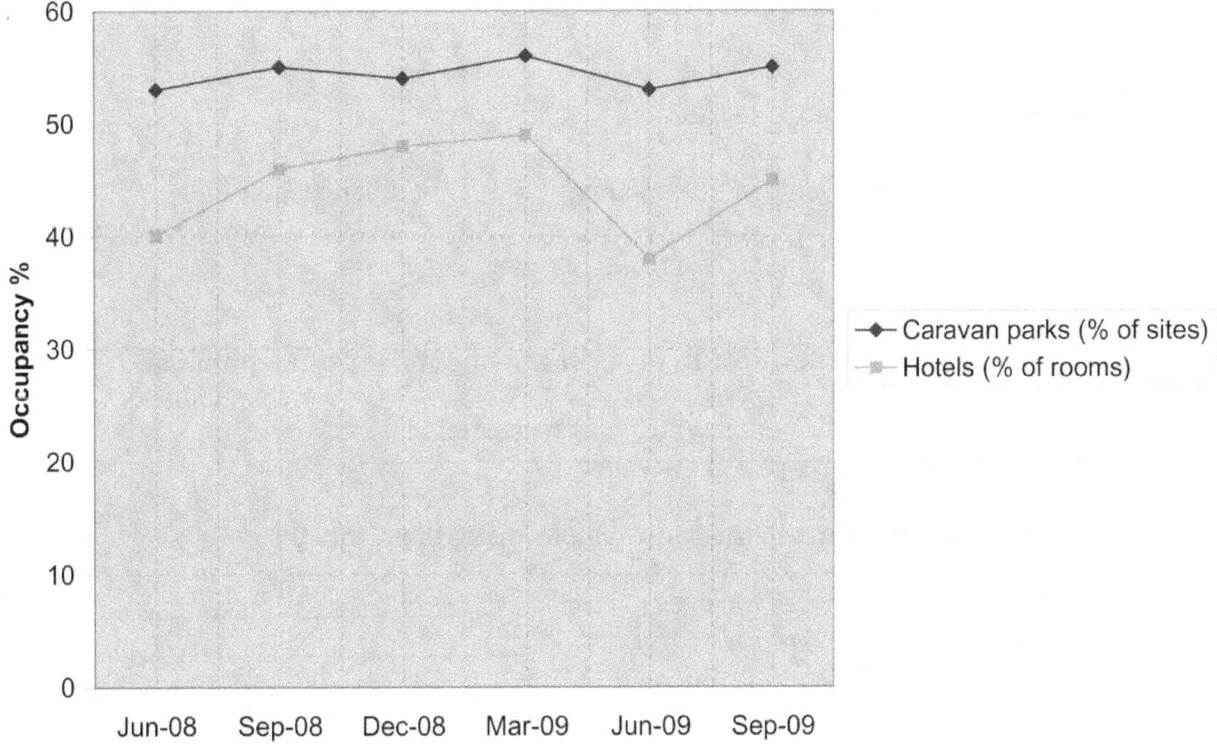

IELTS Writing Task 1 Section

Activities 1 - 2   Get started and build the INTRODUCTION

The answers to all Activities are located in the IELTS Answers section at the end of this book.

1   What is the role of the Introduction?

   a) To outline what the graph shows
   b) To provide an overview of the main trends on the graph
   c) To outline the description of the graph and give an overview of the main trends

2   Correct the tense of the underlined verb in this Introduction

   Introduction

   The graph <u>indicated</u> levels of occupancy of caravan parks and hotels between 2008 and 2009.

Activities 3 - 4   Build the OVERVIEW

3   Comparative adjectives help create an efficient overview sentence. Complete the overview using the most suitable words from the box.

fewer	higher	more	than	less

   Overview

   Overall, it seems that caravan parks had slightly _____ occupancy rates and _____ fluctuation _____ hotels.

4   Writers can sometimes omit words to save time, without damaging grammar.

   Example: '...across the whole period **which was** measured.'
   becomes   '...across the whole period measured'.

   Change these sentence parts in the same way to make them shorter:

   a) ...across the period which was surveyed   _____
   b) ...across the years which were studied   _____
   c) ...across the months which were compared   _____

112   IELTS Test Mastery :: Academic

IELTS Writing Task 1 Section

Activities 5 - 6 Build BODY PARAGRAPH 1
(Describing occupancy rates in caravan parks)

5 Describing graphs involves word forms which express increases and decreases, or no change. Put these verb forms into the spaces correctly:

| peaking | steady | increased | returned | fell back | recovering |

Body Paragraph 1

At the beginning of the period, **in June '08**, the occupancy rate for caravan parks was around 54%. This figure had _____ marginally **by September '08** then _____ a little before _____ at around 57% **in March '09**. **In June '09** it _____ to its original level of 54% before _____ to 56% **by September '09**. Generally, then, occupancy rates were quite _____ across the 15-month period.

6 When describing points of time, correct preposition use is important. Which is the best definition (a-c) of the difference between 'by' and 'in'?

a) 'in' means 'only in that year'; 'by' means in the period of time between two dates.
b) 'in' means 'only in that year'; 'by' means the specific month of that year.
c) 'in' means 'only that month'; 'by' means 'before that month'.

Activities 7 - 8 Build BODY PARAGRAPH 2
(Describing occupancy rates in hotels)

Read Body Paragraph 2 below and answer questions in Activities 7 and 8:

Body Paragraph 2

<u>Turning to</u> hotels, a little more variation was evident. 40% was the hotel occupancy rate in June '08, but then this level increased <u>markedly</u> to around 48% by September of the same year reaching nearly 50% by December. Then the rate dipped <u>significantly</u> to 38% by June '09 before recovering to 45% by September of the same year.

7   At the beginning of Body Paragraph 2, topic shift is signalled by, 'Turning to hotels...'. Which **TWO** expressions below could also be used?

   a) Moving on to consider
   b) According to
   c) In terms of
   d) About

8   'markedly' and 'significantly' are used to show degree of change. Rank these adverbs from the smallest (1) to the largest (4) degree of change.

   substantially (_)   noticeably (_)   marginally (_)   massively (_)

Activity 9   Write a complete report

9   Now write your own report. Spend no more than 20 minutes and write at least 150 words.

   _____

   _____

When you have finished, compare your report to the sample report we have provided in the Treasure Chest.

 *Scan the QR code to access **sample responses for all the activities** in the Treasure Chest or visit https://ielts-blog.com/treasure-chest*

| QUESTION TYPE 4 | Table |

Tables are similar to graphs and are another, very detailed, form of information display. It is important to look carefully across and down the columns so that you pick out the data and key features and changes accurately.

The best strategy is to select the most important features or changes in the data and circle them, including the dates and other specific measures (e.g. $, tonnes, litres and so on). Try to use synonyms to avoid constant repetition of words given in the table.

Again, it is important to write in paragraphs that reflect different aspects of what the table presents. This makes your written answer systematic and orderly. An Introduction and short overview are also important.

Study this Task 1 Table question and complete Activities 1-9 that follow.

Task Question

The table shows the percentage of Australian households with access to computers or the Internet 1998-2000.

Summarise the information by selecting and reporting the key features, and make any relevant comparisons.

Write at least 150 words.

Percentage of Australian households with access to computers/Internet 1998-2000

	access to computers			access to the Internet		
Household income / year	1998	1999	2000	1998	1999	2000
Below $50,000 per year	34	33	37	10	12	21
Above $50,000 per year	69	71	77	34	43	57

IELTS Writing Task 1 Section

Activity 1   Get started and build the INTRODUCTION

 The answers to all Activities are located in the IELTS Answers section at the end of this book.

1   Correct three mistakes in this Introduction.

> **Introduction**
>
> The chart presented data on access to computers and the Internet, in Australia 1998-2000 for two income levels.

Activities 2 - 3   Build the OVERVIEW

2   Which three expressions below best start an Overview <u>formally</u>?

> 'Overall'   'I can see that'   'To summarise'
>
> 'In a nutshell'   'All in all'   'It can be clearly seen that'

3   Choose the comparative expressions to complete the overview neatly.

> upper   more rapidly   much higher   lower

> **Overview**
>
> It can be clearly seen that the _____ income group had _____ access to both the Internet and computers but the _____ income group increased its share of internet access _____.

116   IELTS Test Mastery :: Academic

IELTS Writing Task 1 Section

Activities 4 - 6   Build BODY PARAGRAPH 1
(Describing access to computers)

4   Read Body Paragraph 1. Find the 7-word phrase which introduces the data for the '$50,000+' group, without repeating language used for the 'below $50,000' group.

   Write it here _____

   ### Body Paragraph 1

   The level of access to computers for those on incomes below $50,000 was 34% in 1998, falling marginally to 33% in 1999 before recovering strongly to 37% in 2000. For the above- $50,000 group, the corresponding percentages across the three years were more than double at 69, 71 and 77% respectively.

5   Which expressions in Body Paragraph 1 replace these synonyms?

'salaries'	the writer uses	_____
'dropping'	⇒	_____
'rising again'	⇒	_____
'slightly'	⇒	_____
'equivalent'	⇒	_____
'twice as large'	⇒	_____

6   Accuracy of data is important. Correct the four errors in this same paragraph:

   ### Body Paragraph 1

   The level of access to computers for those on incomes below $50,000 was 34% in 1990, falling marginally to 33% in 1999 before recovering strongly to 87% in 2000. For the above- $5000 group the corresponding percentages across the three years were more than double at 77, 69, and 71% respectively.

IELTS Writing Task 1 Section

Activities 7 - 8   Build BODY PARAGRAPH 2
(Describing access to the internet)

7   Linking expressions build a flowing report. Use items in the box to complete Paragraph 2

> 'Starting from'   'then'   'from'   'the figure increased slightly to'   'to'   'and then to'

Body Paragraph 2

Internet access rates show a slightly different pattern. _____ a low base of 10% in 1998 for the lower income group, _____ 12% in 1999, _____ accelerated to 21% in 2000. For the $50,000 + income group the figures were much higher but the overall increases less dramatic, _____ 34% in 1998, _____ 43% in '99 _____ 57% in 2000.

8   Mechanically listing statistics is too simple. In Body Paragraph 2, find TWO, comparative comments that help to evaluate the data:

Comment 1 _____
Comment 2 _____

Activity 9   Write a complete report

9   Now write your own report. Spend no more than 20 minutes and write at least 150 words.

_____

_____

When you have finished, compare your report to the sample report we have provided in the Treasure Chest.

 *Scan the QR code to access **sample responses** for all the activities in the Treasure Chest or visit https://ielts-blog.com/treasure-chest*

IELTS Writing Task 1 Section

QUESTION TYPE 5 — Chart

Charts are visually simpler to study but can still lead to confusion under test time pressure, as categories can easily be accidentally mixed up and wrong information given in the written response.

The best strategy is to study the horizontal and vertical axes to make clear what they are measuring, circle the categories (e.g. %, age or date) and the key features you will write about. For a systematic answer, decide the topic and content of each paragraph and avoid repetition by using synonyms. A brief introduction and an overview are needed for a fully structured response.

Study this Task 1 Chart question and complete Activities 1-7 that follow.

Task Question

The chart shows coffee consumption by age and percentage of population in Australia in three years - 1995, 2001 and 2004.

Summarise the information by selecting and reporting the key features, and make any relevant comparisons.

Write at least 150 words.

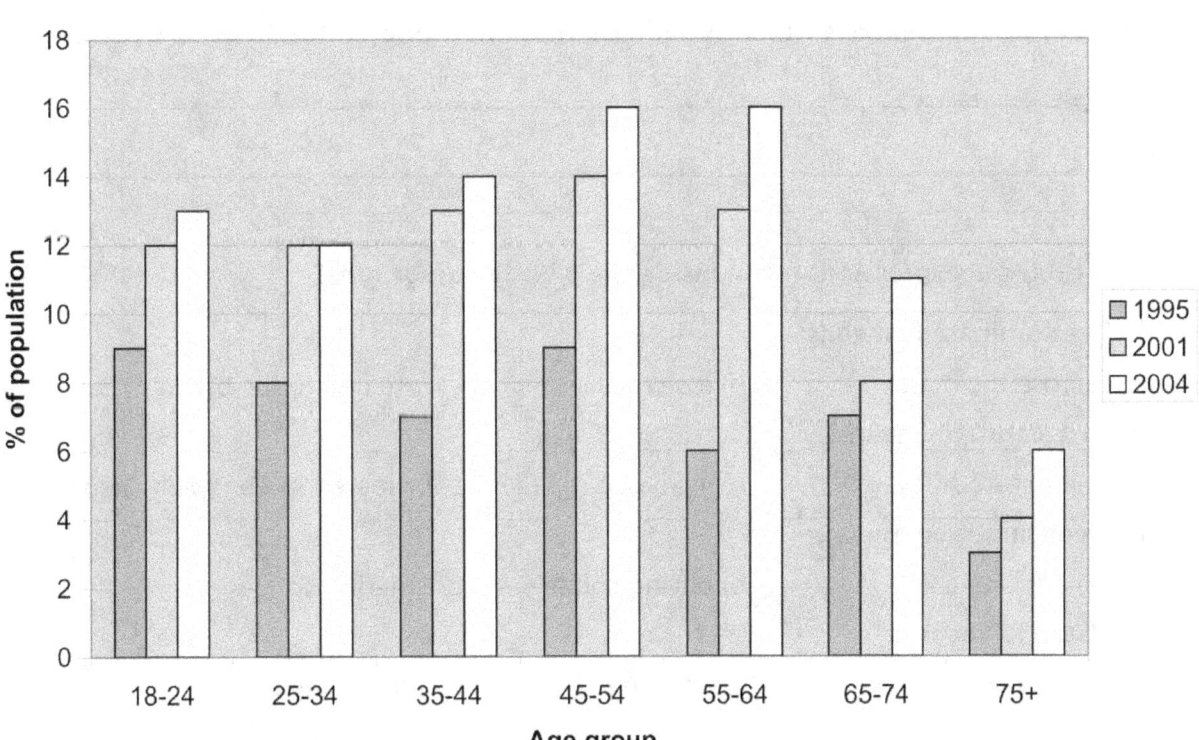

Coffee consumption by age and percent of population

IELTS Writing Task 1 Section

Activity 1 — Get started and build the INTRODUCTION

☑ The answers to all Activities are located in the IELTS Answers section at the end of this book.

1   Look at the chart. Which tense should be used in the Introduction?

   a) present simple (e.g. 'The chart shows')
   b) present continuous (e.g. 'The chart is showing')
   c) present perfect (e.g. 'The chart has shown')

Activity 2 — Build the OVERVIEW

2   Review previous tasks about what goes into an overview, then complete this one:

   Overview

   In general, coffee consumption _____.

Activities 3 - 6 — Build the BODY PARAGRAPHS

3   To create three body paragraphs, is a) or b) a better division of information?

   a)   different age groups   b)   different years

4   Find four age expressions which avoid repetition of '<u>group</u>' in the Activity 6 paragraphs.

   Example: age ranges

   1)_____   3)_____
   2)_____   4)_____

5   What do these expressions mean inside the 3 body paragraphs?

   i) 'predominated' means:
      a) rose the most   b) rose the least   c) rose before the others
   ii) 'accelerated' means:
      a) increased slowly   b) increased rapidly   c) increased more rapidly than before
   iii) 'consumption' means:
      a) drinking coffee   b) buying coffee   c) ordering coffee
   iv) 'steady' means:
      a) reliable   b) unchanged   c) regular increase

IELTS Writing Task 1 Section

6   Don't just quote figures in Task 1, make comparative comments, too. In each of these Body Paragraphs 1, 2 and 3 find one comment (A-F) about the data.

> Taking 1995 first, **(A) it is clear that consumption was fairly similar** for those between 18 and 54 ranging from 7% for the 35-44 group to 9% for the 18-24 and 45-54 age ranges. Older age groups drank less with **(B) 6% in the 55-64 group and 3% in the 75+ cohort.**
>
> By 2001 increases had occurred. The four younger groups had now been joined by the 55-64 group so that **(C) rates ranged among these five age cohorts from 12% up to 14%.** The **(D) older groups showed some increase but at lower rates** — 8% for the 65-74 and 4% for the 75+ category.
>
> In 2004 further increases took place. **(E) The older, middle age ranges predominated**, with 16% of both the 45-54 and 55-64 cohorts drinking coffee, **(F) followed by 14% of 35-44 year-olds and 13% of 18-24 year olds**. The 65–74 year-old group had accelerated to reach 11% with the 25-34 group steady at 12% and the over 75s reaching 6%.

Activity 7   Write a complete report

7   Now write your own report. Spend no more than 20 minutes and write at least 150 words.

_____

_____

When you have finished, compare your report to the sample report we have provided in the Treasure Chest.

 *Scan the QR code to access **sample responses for all the activities** in the Treasure Chest or visit https://ielts-blog.com/treasure-chest*

IELTS Writing Task 1 Section

Boost Your Performance

Improvement starts with personal reflection! Review your most recent Task 1 writing and on this checklist tick those aspects on which you performed well. Those with no ticks indicate where work is still needed!

How did I do?

Good use of time

☐ Systematic routine
☐ No constant clock watching

Stick to the task

☐ Accurate information
☐ Describing patterns and trends, not everything
☐ No personal comments

Appropriate style and tone

☐ No shopping lists
☐ Systematic layout
☐ Formal tone

Which aspects of Task 1 writing are proving difficult for you? Write a few of your thoughts down. Now read through the strategies below, and compare your own writing with our sample responses. Finally, rewrite your original Task 1 answers to build improvements.

If you had difficulties with any of the activities, read these strategies for guidance.

3 Key Strategies to Improve your Task 1 Writing

Strategy I - Good use of time

1. To use time well, follow a systematic routine when practising:

What you should do:	How?	Why?
Stage 1 — understand the task	By studying the wording and data for one to two minutes	To guarantee relevance of your plan and clear structure of the answer
Stage 2 — plan your answer for about two minutes	By writing a quick outline in logical sections	To organise your answer
Stage 3 — write a systematic answer neatly and with clear paragraphing	By following your plan for about 15 minutes.	To make your answer well structured, clear, and easy to read
Stage 4 — check your work quickly	By skim reading; quick word count by counting number of words in one line and then multiply by number of lines (e.g. 10 words x 15 lines = 150)	To pick up any obvious mistakes

Practise writing answers to Task 1 questions with a 20-minute limit. Follow the routine above, and gradually you will manage the restricted time, and will approach the task more professionally.

2. Don't become a 'clock victim'

Some candidates spend too much time counting words or watching the clock. They then lose focus and connection with the actual task. Practise writing Task 1 answers to establish a reliable routine.

Remember, if you are organised, you will create an organised answer. A relevant, organised answer seems professional to the assessor even if it still has some vocabulary and grammar weaknesses.

IELTS Writing Task 1 Section

Strategy II - Stick to the task

1. Accurate information

Whatever material and data are presented to you in Task 1, you need to study and look at each category or number carefully so that your report is accurate. Under pressure of time, candidates sometimes write down incorrect data or leave out key information. This makes their answer incomplete, and lowers their score.

Example 1 – Carelessness (refer to bar chart at the beginning of this chapter, page 119):

Inaccurate information	Accurate information
In 2001 the 35–44 age group had the highest coffee consumption at 15% with the 45–54 and 55–64 cohorts having the same level at 13 percent.	In 2001 the **45–54** age group had the highest coffee consumption at **14%** with the **35–44** and 55–64 cohorts having the same level at 1 percent.

Example 2 – Misunderstanding of measurement categories

Percentage of Australian households with access to computers/Internet 1998-2000

	Access to computers			Access to the Internet		
Household income/year	1998	1999	2000	1998	1999	2000
Below $50,000 per year	34	33	37	10	12	21
Above $50,000 per year	69	71	77	34	43	57

Inaccurate information	Accurate information
In 1998, among men with $50,000 in income 34 lived in houses with access to a computer and 10 to the internet.	In 1998, **34% of households** with an annual salary of **less than $50, 000** had access to a computer, and **10 percent** to the internet.

2. Write about important patterns and trends - not everything

The Task 1 question usually asks you to summarise and report main trends. This means building an overview of the data and then selecting the key information. There isn't time to write about everything so learn how to identify, organise, compare, contrast, and finally, combine the key information.

Example

Too much detail	Better version
In 2001 in the 18–24 age group 12 percent drank coffee, in the 25–34 age group also 12 percent. In the 35–44 age group 13 percent drank coffee, and 14% in the 45–54 age group. In the 55–64 age group less, 8 percent drank coffee and finally only 4 percent of the 75+ group drank coffee.	In 2001, younger and middle-aged age groups had similar coffee drinking patterns at 12 percent (younger) and 13/14 percent (middle aged), while the two, older age groups drank much less coffee at 4–8%.

3. Avoid personal comments about the statistical material

Some candidates start to give their own explanations for why the data has changed, even though this is not in the graph and not part of the task.

Example

*Watching TV probably increased more for young people in the period 2005–2010 **because parents were too busy** to do other things with their children.*

Every word has to count in Task 1 as you have so little time. Writing information that is not in the diagram or graph is irrelevant. Your task is reporting data, not guessing possible causes of it.

IELTS Writing Task 1 Section

Strategy III - Appropriate style and tone

1. Avoid 'shopping lists'

Some candidates see information on a graph or table and just repeat it without any selection, comparison or synthesis.

Example

Report 1

In Belonia in 2001 unemployment was 20%; in 2002 it was 30%, in 2003 it increased to 40%; in 2004 it was steady at 40%; In Celonia in 2001 it was 20%, in 2002 it was 10%, in 2002 it decreased to 5% and in 2004 it rose to 20%'

Report 2

Unemployment in Belonia **increased steadily** from 20 to 40% between 2001 and 2003, at which point it **remained stead**y. In Celonia, **howeve**r, the percentage without work **halved each year** from 20% in 2001 down to 5% in 2003, then rose again to 20%.

Report 2 has the better style of reporting as it evaluates the changes, it doesn't simply list them.

If you identify trends and patterns in statistical data instead of just making mechanical lists, you are showing you can interpret and evaluate information in terms of what is more/less important. Though not strictly a language skill this indicates mature, critical thinking.

2. Use a systematic layout

Use an Introduction/overview/body paragraphs format, with each body paragraph dealing with a clear and distinct area of information.

A well-organised and logically structured report seems more professional and the assessor can read your report more easily. This has a strong, positive impact. A report without clear and logical sections makes the information much harder to read.

Example

The report below has no paragraphing:

The chart shows a three-year, percentage pattern for coffee consumption among different age groups in Australia. In general, coffee consumption increased for all age groups but more rapidly for the middle and older age ranges.
Taking 1995 first, it is clear that consumption was fairly similar for those between 18 and 54 ranging from 7% for the 35-44 group to 9% for the 18-24 and 45-54 age ranges. Older age groups drank less with 6% in the 55-64 group and 3% in the 75+ cohort.
By 2001 increases had occurred. The four younger groups had now been joined by the 55-64 group so that rates ranged among these five age cohorts from 12% up to 14%. The older groups showed some increase but at lower rates — 8% for the 65-74 and 4% for the 75+ category.
In 2004 further increases occurred. The older middle age ranges predominated, with 16% of both the 45-54 and 55-64 cohorts drinking coffee, followed by 14% of 35-44 year-olds and 13% of 18-24 year olds. The 65-74 year-old group had accelerated to reach 11% with the 25-34 group steady at 12% and the over 75s reaching 6%.

Compare the above with this better version which has clear paragraphing:

The chart shows a three-year, percentage pattern for coffee consumption among different age groups in Australia. **(Introduction)**

In general, coffee consumption increased for all age groups but more rapidly for the middle and older age ranges. **(Overview)**

Taking 1995 first, it is clear that consumption was fairly similar for those between 18 and 54 ranging from 7% for the 35-44 group to 9% for the 18-24 and 45-54 age ranges. Older age groups drank less with 6% in the 55-64 group and 3% in the 75+ cohort. **(Summary of 1995)**

By 2001 increases had occurred. The four younger groups had now been joined by the 55-64 group so that rates ranged among these five age cohorts from 12% up to 14%. The older groups showed some increase but at lower rates — 8% for the 65-74 and 4% for the 75+ category. **(Summary of 2001)**

In 2004 further increases occurred. The older middle age ranges predominated, with 16% of both the 45-54 and 55-64 cohorts drinking coffee, followed by 14% of 35-44 year-olds and 13% of 18-24 year olds. The 65-74 year-old group had accelerated to reach 11% with the 25-34 group steady at 12% and the over 75s reaching 6%. **(Summary of 2004)**

3. Use a formal tone

A professional writing style is formal in tone and economical in style. It maximises clarity of information and brings together key information effectively by effective use of appropriate formal vocabulary and sentence links.

The use of an appropriate tone and style adds to the assessor's belief in your professionalism, even if there are still a few grammatical errors. This builds a positive impression. So compare these expressions:

Expression 1	Expression 2
big increase	significant/substantial increase
went up quickly	rose rapidly
got suddenly bigger	increased dramatically
went down a lot	decreased significantly
go a bit higher	increased marginally
stayed the same	remained unchanged/stable
quite a lot of students	a substantial number of students
pretty much the same	broadly similar

The second expression in each case is more formal, establishing a professional tone for reporting information. In this writing context, the first expression seems more like spoken English.

Key Problems with Language in Writing Task 1

Think about the language you use when answering Task 1. How many of these 7 problems with language have you had in your recent Task 1 writing?

Language problems

Problem 1: Incorrect use of Word Forms (adjective/noun/adverb)

Problem 2: Inaccurate Verb Tenses

Problem 3: Lack of agreement between Subject and Verb

Problem 4: Poor use of Full Stops

Problem 5: Missing out important words

Problem 6: Careless Spelling

Problem 7: Repeating, repeating, repeating

 Scan the QR code to download the **solutions for these problems** from the Treasure Chest or visit https://ielts-blog.com/treasure-chest

WRITING TASK 2 PRACTICE

WHAT'S INSIDE:

- **Practise the Question Types**
- **Boost Your Performance**

IELTS Writing Task 2 Section

Practise the IELTS Writing Task 2 Types

QUESTION TYPE 1   **Choose your point of view and support it**

This type requires you to agree, partly agree or disagree with the point of view stated in the task.

The best strategy is to build your answer by systematic use of paragraphs - an introduction to the task, body paragraphs which first discuss the view opposite to yours, and then develop your own view, and, finally, a summarising conclusion.

It is helpful to write an outline plan (with your ideas, useful words and so on for each paragraph) before writing your actual response. This can be referred to, but also crossed out and underlined so that it is clearly separate from, and not seen as part of, your actual answer.

Study this Task 2 and complete Activities 1-25 that follow

> **Shopping is dangerous because it makes people selfish, and careless with money.**
>
> **Do you agree or disagree?**
>
> *Give reasons for your answer and include any relevant examples from your own knowledge or experience.*
>
> *Write at least 250 words*

IELTS Writing Task 2 Section

Activities 1 - 2   Identify the KIND OF RESPONSE required

The answers to all Activities are located in the IELTS Answers section at the end of this book.

1   'Do you agree or disagree?' means that you need to...

   a) choose and defend one of these views (Yes, I agree OR No, I don't agree) based on the nature of your own viewpoint.
   b) write to show you both agree and disagree equally.
   c) do what you like as long as you talk about shopping.

2   Which word (a-c) from the task indicates your answer should support ONE view only?

   a) money   b) because   c) or

Activities 3 - 5   Plan your answer

3   How many paragraphs will work well in this type of essay?

   a) 4 (Introduction, 2 body paragraphs, Conclusion).
   b) 5 (Introduction, 3 body paragraphs, Conclusion).
   c) 3 (Introduction, 1 body paragraph, Conclusion).

4   What's the best thing to do next?

   a) Start writing.
   b) Write down some key ideas to support and oppose your viewpoint.
   c) Decide on your viewpoint and then write down some ideas.

5   About how many sentences seem reasonable in the Introduction?

   a) 2–3 sentences   b) 3–5 sentences   c) 6–7 sentences

IELTS Test Mastery :: Academic

IELTS Writing Task 2 Section

Activities 6 - 9   Build the INTRODUCTION

Read this Introduction before completing the activities that follow.

> **Introduction**
>
> <u>Shopping has become a popular leisure activity in many countries in the developed world, but it has hidden risks.</u> Advertising and credit cards have both contributed to making shopping more dangerous by encouraging self-centred attitudes and irresponsible financial habits. I strongly believe that shopping has become too tempting and harmful for many consumers, who are likely to make poor decisions with lasting consequences.

6 What's the main purpose of the first sentence of the Introduction?

   a) To start by talking generally about the overall topic of shopping
   b) To stop the opinion sentence (2) from being the first one.
   c) To raise the topic of shopping and make a 'bridge' into the writer's point of view.

7 Which 3 synonyms in the Introduction avoid using these words from the task statement?

   people   _____
   selfish   _____
   careless _____

8 Using 'is likely to' in Task 2 is helpful as it shows less certainty than future tense 'will'.

   Rewrite these sentences, using 'likely' to express less certainty:

   a) Shopping will grow in popularity.   Shopping is _____
   b) Shopping will never die out.   Shopping is not _____
   c) Overspending will cause problems.   Overspending is _____
   d) Shopping will never bring happiness.   It is highly un_____that_____

9 Complete new sentences of similar meaning but in a less personal style:

   a) Shoppers are selfish.
      Shopping makes _____ _____ (2 words)

   b) Consumers are dangerous when they go shopping.
      Shopping makes _____ _____ (2 words)

   c) People spend unwisely at the shops.
      Shopping makes _____ _____ _____ (3 words)

   d) Shoppers lack self-discipline.
      Shopping makes _____ _____ (2 words)

IELTS Writing Task 2 Section

Activities 10 - 11   Build BODY PARAGRAPH 1

Read Body Paragraph 1 before completing the activities that follow.

> **Body Paragraph 1**
>
> **Not all shoppers are poor money managers.** As costs and bills are increasing constantly, many families have developed excellent **financial skills, enabling them** to pay their bills and shop fairly for every family member. There are also **financial advisers available** to help develop such skills.

10   What is the purpose of the (topic) sentence 1 in Body Paragraph 1?

   a) It enables the writer to establish that not all shoppers are rich.
   b) It enables the writer briefly to discuss his central point of view.
   c) It establishes that there is a point of view that is different from the writer's.

11   Use relative clauses to complete these economical sentences from Paragraph 1 differently.

   a) Many families have developed excellent financial skills which_____.
   b) There are also financial advisers, who_____.

Activities 12 - 15   Build BODY PARAGRAPH 2

Read Body Paragraph 2 before completing the activities that follow.

> **Body Paragraph 2**
>
> **Advertising is one of the key reasons why people think more selfishly.** Many adverts depict glamorous lives where certain products are shown as essential to a sense of being successful, attractive or fashionable. Ordinary consumers are persuaded at a psychological level by advertisers and made to feel inadequate if they don't have products such as cosmetics, brand name goods, new shoes or cars. This creates willing shoppers who put their desire for personal appearance and wellbeing above their sense of community welfare.

12   The central idea in the first (topic) sentence for further development is...

   a) selfishness   b) reasons   c) advertising

IELTS Writing Task 2 Section

13 A good sentence construction for explaining something in a Task 2 is:

'_____ is one of the key reasons why _____'.

Complete these sentences appropriately using your own explanations:

a) The desire for a good job is one of the key reasons why _____
b) The wish for a more exciting life is one of the principal reasons why _____
c) The hope for more money is one of the major reasons why _____
d) _____ is one of the main reasons why marriage is still popular.

14 Which higher-level expressions in Paragraph 2 improve these simpler options?

Simpler option	Higher level expression in Body Paragraph 2
show (verb)	_____
shoppers	_____
not good enough	_____
goods	_____
wish (noun)	_____
look (noun)	_____
feeling good	_____
social good	_____

15 In which <u>two, main ways</u> do adjectives in Paragraph 2 help raise a test score?

a) They add variety and interest.
b) They enable the writer to show greater range of vocabulary use.
c) They help build the viewpoint.

Activities 16 - 20   Build BODY PARAGRAPH 3

Read Body Paragraph 3 before completing the activities that follow.

Body Paragraph 3

The advent of the credit card has encouraged consumers to be **far less** cautious about their money. Credit cards are part of the 'cashless society', in which more and more transactions don't require actual cash. **The result is that money becomes** more abstract and, via constantly increasing credit limits, consumers can pretend to have money that they don't actually possess, and can buy things that they want immediately, but before they have really earned the money to pay for them. **This** often leads to having to face constant debt and to a sense of life being lived 'here and now' rather than linked to building a stable future.

16 Language choices which grade the amount of change are important.

Example in Body Paragraph 3: '**far less** cautious'

Complete these sentences with 'less' or 'more':

a) Most teenagers read **considerably** _____ than they did in the past.
b) Women are **far** _____ intelligent than men (You choose!)
c) Airline fares are **much** _____ expensive nowadays.
d) IELTS is **considerably** _____ popular than it used to be.

17 'The result is that....' is a good phrase to use in Task 2.

Which phrase (a-d) could NOT appropriately replace it in Body Paragraph 3?

a) As a consequence, money becomes...
b) This results in money becoming...
c) An outcome of this is that money becomes...
d) Money becomes a result that...

18 Guess how many sentences Body Paragraph 3 has, then check.

a) 6   b) 8   c) 4

19 Use of 'This...' in Paragraph 3 prevents repetition. What does 'this' <u>refer back</u> to here?

a) earning money
b) buying things immediately
c) pretending to have money

20 Judge these effects of long sentences as either + (Positive) or – (Negative).

a) Long sentences can aid reading flow as the writer's ideas are connected more fluently **(+ / –)**
b) Long sentences may put extra pressure on memory **(+ / –)**
c) Long sentences enable more flexible use of connecting expressions **(+ / –)**
d) Long sentences may reduce clarity of ideas **(+ / –)**

Review the length and clarity of your own sentences when you practise Task 2.

Judging when or when not to use long sentences improves as your writing develops.

IELTS Writing Task 2 Section

Activities 21 - 23   Build the CONCLUSION

Read the Conclusion before completing the activities that follow.

> **Conclusion**
>
> All in all then, shopping has become all too tempting for many consumers, who want to feel good and feel rewarded perhaps for their ever-busier working lives. Advertising feeds this desire and credit cards feed instant gratification. I firmly believe that the consequences of these trends **may well be** harmful for families and society, including egocentric attitudes and financial recklessness.

21   The purpose of this Conclusion seems to be:

a) to summarise the writer's point of view and express their opinion.
b) to offer some new information.
c) to give the opposite point of view.

22   Complete these two expressions with two, intensifying words from the Conclusion:

_____ _____ tempting   _____ - _____ working lives

Now put these expressions into the sentences below

| all too | ever-growing | far too | never-ending | ever-busier |

a) It is _____ easy to spend money, and _____ difficult to save it.
b) Internet crime is an _____ problem.
c) Working lives are becoming _____.
d) There seems to be a _____ rise in the price of food.

23   'May well be' makes an opinion seem more cautious than 'will be'.

Which three expressions (a-e) seem similarly cautious?

a) will definitely be...   d) can't fail but be...
b) could easily be...   e) may turn out to be...
c) might well be...

Activity 24   Write a complete essay

24   Now write your own essay. Spend no more than 40 minutes and write at least 250 words.

Use the 5-paragraph structure, ensuring each body paragraph has a clear first (topic) sentence identifying the topic to be developed as those paragraphs are built.

_____

_____

When you have finished, compare your essay to the sample essay we have provided in the Treasure Chest.

 *Scan the QR code to access the **sample response** for this essay in the Treasure Chest or visit https://ielts-blog.com/treasure-chest*

IELTS Writing Task 2 Section

QUESTION TYPE 2   Present a two-sided Discussion

This type requires you to discuss 2 sides of an argument or 2 points of view, and explain which one you personally agree (or partly agree) with, and why.

The best strategy is to build your answer by systematic use of paragraphs - an introduction to the task that also includes your opinion, three body paragraphs which discuss the two sides of the argument, and then your own view, and a summarising conclusion.

It is helpful to write an outline plan (with your ideas, useful words and so on for each paragraph) before writing your actual response. This can be referred to, but also crossed out and underlined so that it is clearly separate from, and not seen as part of, your actual answer.

Study this Task 2 and complete Activities 1 - 20 that follow

> **Some say you should always marry for love; others say that in an uncertain world it's wiser to marry for money.**
>
> **Discuss both points of view and give your own opinion.**
>
> *Give reasons for your answer and include any relevant examples from your own knowledge or experience.*
>
> *Write at least 250 words*

Activities 1 - 3   Identify the KIND OF RESPONSE required

The answers to all Activities are located in the IELTS Answers section at the end of this book.

1 This type of essay requires you to...

   a) choose one point of view only.
   b) give your own opinion on both points of view.
   c) talk about both points of view neutrally, then give your own personal view.

2 The main topic is...

   a) marriage as an institution
   b) the basis of marriage
   c) links between love and money

3 Is a) or b) the better description of the points of view for discussion?

   a) whether you should only get married because you love someone or whether you should only get married for financial advantage.
   b) whether it's more sensible to get married for love or more sensible to marry for financial benefit given the modern world's uncertainties.

Activities 4 - 5   Plan your answer

4   How many paragraphs seem the most logical for this type of essay?

   a) 5   b) 4   c) 6

5   What's the best thing to do next?

   a) Decide which part of the essay will go into which paragraph.
   b) Note some key ideas for the main paragraphs.
   c) Write the introduction.

Activities 6 - 8   Build the INTRODUCTION

Read this Introduction before completing the activities that follow.

> **Introduction**
>
> The issue of love and marriage has been part of most cultures for centuries. With economic uncertainties, pure romance is under challenge, but can still find a way to maintain its vital place in marriage. While some may prioritise financial stability, I firmly believe that love is the foundation of a meaningful marriage, as it provides emotional fulfilment and strengthens relationships.

6   Which statement is correct? Choose from (a-c).

   The Introduction:

   a) introduces the topic and expresses the writer's own opinion.
   b) talks generally but doesn't express the writer's own opinion.
   c) focuses on historical and economic facts.

7   In the Introduction, find more economical phrases than either a) or b) below:

   a) Some people have jobs but don't have a trust in the future of their jobs or their money.
   b) True and real love has got many things which are trying to make it weaker.

   Shorter phrase: a) _____   b) _____

8   Choose the best expression to complete (a-d) using either 'topic', 'issue' or 'problem'.

   a) Poverty is a _____ facing many nations.
   b) Whether or not to have children is an important _____ these days.
   c) Beauty is a frequently discussed _____.
   d) Climate change is one of the most serious _____ in the world today.

IELTS Writing Task 2 Section

Activities 9 - 12   Build BODY PARAGRAPH 1

Read Body Paragraph 1 before completing the activities that follow.

> **Body Paragraph 1**
>
> Most couples in western societies **would claim that** they still marry for love. **This is because** they are usually free to choose a life partner. Love provides a strong emotional bond between men and women, and continues into adulthood the strong feelings that most children receive from their parents. **It is well known that** a strong marriage based on love gives each partner the strength, stability and emotional security to pursue their careers with confidence. Lonely, unloved individuals, **often seem to** struggle more in every part of their lives.

9 Verb forms that are less direct often seem more considered. Compare:
   (A) 'Most couples **would claim that they marry** for love' with
   (B) 'Most couples **marry** for love'

   Sentence A communicates a sense of doubt. Which <u>three</u> options (a-e) also do this?

   Most couples...
   a) want to get...
   b) clearly want to believe...
   c) only get married...
   d) are probably convinced...
   e) would no doubt assert...

10 'This is because...' is a neat explanation, linked to its preceding sentence.

   Match sentence 1 with its appropriate sentence 2:

Sentence 1	Sentence 2
a) Many women today marry later.	i) **This is because** neither partner can always have their own way.
b) The number of divorces is rising.	ii) **This is because** many couples want celebrity-style weddings.
c) Getting married is now very expensive.	iii) **This is because** they want to build their careers first, just like men do.
d) Marriage involves compromise	iv) **This is because** couples get bored too easily and lack commitment.

11 'It is well known that...' helps a writer to claim a general truth.

   Example: 'It is well known that a strong marriage based on love gives each partner...'

   Write your own ending to complete these sentences in a suitable way:

   a) It is well known that women _____.
   b) It is well known that celebrities _____.
   c) It is well known that divorce _____.

IELTS Writing Task 2 Section

12 'often seem(s)' instead of a simple verb stops the writer appearing too assertive.

   Compare:
   'Lonely individuals struggle more in their lives' **with**
   'Lonely individuals <u>often seem</u> to struggle more in their lives'

   Change these verb forms using 'often seem':

   a) Men are less committed to marriage than women.
   b) Women are more romantic than men.
   c) Couples today struggle to keep their marriage alive.
   d) A child knows when parents are not happy.

Activities 13 - 15   Build BODY PARAGRAPH 2

Read Body Paragraph 2 before completing the activities that follow.

> **Body Paragraph 2**
>
> At the same time, **it cannot be denied that** economic realities have made everyone more practical. Seeking a partner who has good **career prospects** is a wise and sensible thing to do as it provides a better basis for economic stability within a family. So, **it is quite likely that** the modern marriage may unconsciously be based on both love and money, in the sense that a suitable person to fall in love with may tend to be someone with a well-paid job.

13 Writers often use an introductory phrase to strengthen their viewpoint.

   Example: '**It cannot be denied that** economic realities have made everyone more practical.'

   Add your own viewpoint about marriage to these introductory phrases:

   a) It cannot be denied that _____.
   b) It is certainly the case that _____.
   c) There is little doubt that _____.
   d) It is undeniable that _____.

14 **Using noun + noun helps to communicate information economically.**
   Example: 'Prospects of having a career' = 'career prospects'.

   Put these phrases into a neat, noun + noun form:

   a) A cake eaten at a wedding =   _____.
   b) A ceremony in which you get married =   _____.
   c) Your partner in marriage =   _____.
   d) An opportunity to get a job =   _____.

IELTS Test Mastery :: Academic

IELTS Writing Task 2 Section

15   Expressing degrees of probability is helpful when making a prediction in writing.

   Example: '...it is quite likely that the modern marriage may...'

   Arrange these predictions from the most likely (1) to the least likely (4):

   a) It is highly likely that   _____   c) It is quite likely that   _____
   b) It is very unlikely that   _____   d) There is little likelihood that   _____

Activities 16 - 18   Build BODY PARAGRAPH 3

Read Body Paragraph 3 before completing the activities that follow.

> **Body Paragraph 3**
>
> My own view is that love should, as they say, 'conquer all'. Without love we, as human beings, are lost to ourselves and lost to others. **Most surveys show that** happiness is **based on** strong, positive relationships **not on** wealth. Marriage should be based on a strong, emotional relationship **so that** children will grow up being loved, and the cycle of love can continue.

16   Adding supporting evidence makes your viewpoint stronger.
   Example: 'Most surveys show that...'

   Which of these phrases seem similar in meaning to the example from Body Paragraph 3?

   a) Much research evidence indicates that...
   b) I have a viewpoint which shows that...
   c) Most of the evidence points to the fact that...
   d) I really believe that...

17   Contrasting two points of view economically is useful.
   Example: 'Love is **based on** respect, **not on** wealth'

   Choose expressions from the box to complete these sentences:

   | proximity | commitment | taste | reputation | infatuation | nutrition |

   a) Marriage should be **based on** _____, not on _____.
   b) Choosing a university should be **based on** _____, not on _____.
   c) A good diet should be **based on** _____, not on _____.

18 Using 'so that' to express purpose is effective in formal writing.
    Example: 'Marriage exists <u>so that</u> children can grow up in a stable family'

    Complete these complex sentences of purpose with your own ideas

    a) Children go to school **so that** they can_____.
    b) Couples get married **so that** they can_____.
    c) Young married couples save **so that** they can _____.

Activity 19   Build the CONCLUSION

Read the Conclusion before completing the activity that follows.

> **Conclusion**
>
> **To summarise,** while financial security may influence modern marriages, I firmly believe that love is the key to a happy and fulfilling life.

19 Which 3 expressions below could replace 'To summarise,...' ?

    a) All in all   b) Finally   c) After all   d) To sum up   e) Lastly   f) Summing up

Activity 20   Write a complete essay

20 Now write your own essay. Spend no more than 40 minutes and write at least 250 words.

    Use the 5-paragraph structure, ensuring each body paragraph has a clear first (topic) sentence identifying the topic to be developed as those paragraphs are built.

    _____

    _____

When you have finished, compare your essay to the sample essay we have provided in the Treasure Chest.

*Scan the QR code to access the **sample response for this essay** in the Treasure Chest or visit https://ielts-blog.com/treasure-chest*

IELTS Writing Task 2 Section

QUESTION TYPE 3 — Discuss Advantages & Disadvantages

This type requires you to discuss the advantages and disadvantages of a given situation or viewpoint.

The best strategy is to build your answer by systematic use of paragraphs - an introduction to the task that says what you will address in your answer, two body paragraphs which discuss advantages and disadvantages with supporting examples and a summarising conclusion (without too much repetition).

It is helpful to write an outline plan (with your ideas, useful words and so on for each paragraph) before writing your actual response. This can be referred to, but also crossed out and underlined so that it is clearly separate from, and not seen as part of, your actual answer.

Study this Task 2 and complete Activities 1-10 that follow

In some countries older people are being encouraged to work longer and not to retire.

Do the advantages of working beyond retirement age outweigh the disadvantages?

Give reasons for your answer and include any relevant examples from your own knowledge or experience.

Write at least 250 words

Activity 1 — Identify the KIND OF RESPONSE required

 The answers to all Activities are located in the IELTS Answers section at the end of this book.

1. In this type of essay you need to discuss:

    a) advantages only.
    b) both advantages and disadvantages.
    c) disadvantages only, if you think there are no advantages.

Activity 2 — Plan your answer

2. How many paragraphs will work well in this type of essay?

    a) 3 (Introduction, 1 body paragraph, Conclusion).
    b) 5 (Introduction, 3 body paragraphs, Conclusion).
    c) 4 (Introduction, 2 body paragraphs, Conclusion).

Activity 3   Build the INTRODUCTION

Read this Introduction before completing the activity that follows.

Introduction

The retirement age is no longer fixed in many societies. As a result, some workers now prefer to delay retirement, while others choose to leave earlier. Prolonging work past retirement age allows people to maintain routines, stay socially active, and build financial security, but it can also cause physical strain, limit leisure time, and block opportunities for younger workers. In my opinion, the drawbacks outweigh the benefits, as later years should focus on health and personal fulfilment rather than work.

3   Which words in the Introduction avoid repeating these words in the task:

   a) advantages and disadvantages   _____
   b) working beyond   _____

Activities 4 - 5   Build BODY PARAGRAPH 1

Body Paragraph 1

Some benefit can be easily identified. One clear advantage of delaying retirement is that it enable the maintenance of well-established daily routines. With age regularity seem to become more important psychologically and physically. A second benefit is that most work provide opportunities for social contact with groups and individual. Again, this is beneficial to a sense of wellbeing and usefulness.

Read Body Paragraph 1 before completing the activities that follow.

4   How many different advantages are there in Body Paragraph 1?

   a) 1   b) 3   c) 2

5   Five words in Body Paragraph 1 need an 's' at the end. Write them correctly below:

   1. _____
   2. _____
   3. _____
   4. _____
   5. _____

IELTS Writing Task 2 Section

Activities 6 - 8   Build BODY PARAGRAPH 2

Read Body Paragraph 2 before completing the activities that follow.

> **Body Paragraph 2**
>
> On other hand, working past retirement age is not always a good thing. Physically, full time job can be demanding especially these days, and workers of retirement age are starting to lose their physical strength. Secondly, after forty or more years of work, there is less time remaining to pursue those activities and trips for which there was never enough time. Many retired people, for example, undertake ambitious trips worldwide, while they are still healthy. Finally, staying on past retirement potentially robs younger workers of opportunities for promotion, or may prevent young workers from actually entering workforce.

6   How many <u>disadvantages</u> (a-c) are mentioned in Paragraph 2? How many provide <u>examples</u>?

   Disadvantages: a) 5   b) 4   c) 3
   Supporting example(s): a) 1   b) 2   c) 3

7   The writer missed 'the' (twice) and 'a' (once) in Paragraph 2. Write the complete forms here:

   1. _____
   2. _____
   3. _____

8   Which words does the writer use to improve these simpler choices?

   a) hard   _____
   b) left   _____
   c) go on   _____
   d) stop   _____

Activity 9 Build the CONCLUSION

Read the Conclusion before completing the activity that follows.

> **Conclusion**
>
> In conclusion, while continuing to work later in life offers benefits such as maintaining routines, social engagement, and financial security, I firmly believe the drawbacks outweigh the benefits. Prioritising health, enjoying personal fulfilment, and creating opportunities for younger generations should take precedence over prolonging work in later life.

9   What does this conclusion achieve? Choose a, b or c:

   a) It repeats some advantages and disadvantages.
   b) It briefly summarises a key point from each paragraph and states the writer's opinion.
   c) It offers some new ideas.

Activity 10 Write a complete essay

10   Now write your own essay. Spend no more than 40 minutes and write at least 250 words.

   Use the 5-paragraph structure, ensuring each body paragraph has a clear first (topic) sentence identifying the topic to be developed as those paragraphs are built.

   _____

   _____

When you have finished, compare your essay to the sample essay we have provided in the Treasure Chest.

 *Scan the QR code to access the **sample response for this essay** in the Treasure Chest or visit https://ielts-blog.com/treasure-chest*

IELTS Writing Task 2 Section

QUESTION TYPE 4   Explain & Offer Solutions or Consequences

This type requires you to explain the reasons why the situation in the task prompt has arisen, and how it can be solved, or what consequences it gives rise to.

The best strategy is to build your answer by systematic use of paragraphs - an introduction to the task that says what you will address in your answer, two body paragraphs which discuss the first and second questions in the task prompt with supporting examples and a summarising conclusion (without too much repetition).

It is helpful to write an outline plan (with your ideas, useful words and so on for each paragraph) before writing your actual response. This can be referred to, but also crossed out and underlined so that it is clearly separate from, and not seen as part of, your actual answer.

Study this Task 2 and complete Activities 1-8 that follow.

Family life is suffering because of the pressure of work.

Why is this happening?
What is the most important way to improve the quality of family life?

Give reasons for your answer and include any relevant examples from your own knowledge or experience.

Write at least 250 words

Activity 1   Identify the KIND OF RESPONSE required

 The answers to all Activities are located in the IELTS Answers section at the end of this book.

1   In this task type you should:

   a) Say whether you agree or not with the first statement.
   b) Explain why the situation exists, and what to do to make the situation better.
   c) Talk about ways in which work pressure is increasing and how to improve this problem.

Activities 2 - 3   Plan your answer

2   How many paragraphs are ideal between Introduction and Conclusion?

   a) 3   b) 1   c) 2

IELTS Writing Task 2 Section

3   Imagine this question is on your IELTS test paper. Write down some ideas below:

Why is family life suffering?	Most important way to improve family life

Activity 4 Build the INTRODUCTION

Read this Introduction before completing the activity that follows.

Introduction

In many countries both husbands and wives work full time. Unfortunately, this sometimes means that they have less time to spend with their children and may have to put even very young children into care. Family life is suffering because financial demands and tight work schedules reduce the time families spend together. It seems to me that the key to making family life better is to prioritise family values in government policies and workplace practices.

4   Which phrases replace these in the task question, to avoid repetition?

In the task question	In the Introduction
a) pressure of work	_____
b) the most important way to improve the quality of family life	_____

Activity 5 Build BODY PARAGRAPH 1

Read Body Paragraph 1 before completing the activity that follows.

Body Paragraph 1

There is a range of reasons why the deterioration in family life can be linked to the work situation. In the first place, employers are becoming so cost conscious that they reduce their workforces as much as they can to reduce costs. Consequently, the other workers then may have to work longer hours to cover an increased workload. Similarly, workers often feel pressure to get better qualifications in order to remain employable. As a result, they enrol for part-time courses which then have to be completed in their leisure time, thus robbing them of valuable hours with their children. Finally, it seems that work is speeding up. In other words, electronic technology saves time in some ways, but increases management's expectations of what employees can be expected to achieve within a working day. This can mean that workers have to take work home in order to keep up. Taken together, such issues build pressure at home and families spend less time together.

IELTS Writing Task 2 Section

5 Match each linking expression (a-j) on the left with one on the right that has a similar meaning or function.

Alternative expressions	Expressions from Body Paragraph 1
a) First of all,...	In other words
b) Lastly,...	Taken together
c) All in all...	This can mean that
d) So...	In the first place
e) In the same way,...	Consequently
f) Thereby...	Similarly
g) Putting it another way,...	so.... that
h) The result of this is that...	As a result
i) such that...	Finally
j) This can lead to a situation in which...	thus

Activity 6   Build BODY PARAGRAPH 2

Read Body Paragraph 2 before completing the activity that follows.

Body Paragraph 2

Line
1 There is only one real key to changing the situation. This would involve a **big** change
2 in social values such that the family and the upbringing of children would be viewed
3 by governments and companies as the **biggest** social task. Then, work practices and
4 government policies would be built around this **good** value. As a result, workers would
5 be protected and given **good** time for the **big** role of socialisation and the building of
6 strong, loving and **good** relationships with their children.

6 Upgrade the simpler language (a-f) from the paragraph, using the adjectives in the box.

| fundamental | vital | important |
| sufficient | empathetic | most significant |

Expression in Body Paragraph 2	Appropriate, higher level alternative ?
a) big change (line 1)	_____ change
b) biggest social task (line 3)	_____ social task
c) good value (line 4)	_____ value
d) good time (line 5)	_____ time
e) big role (line 5)	_____ role
f) good relationships (line 6)	_____ relationships

Activities 7 - 8   Build the CONCLUSION

Read the Conclusion before completing the activity that follows.

> **Conclusion**
>
> To conclude, economic pressures are leading to harder and longer work and **this** is reducing shared family time. A major change in social values is the key to changing **this** situation.

7   **Using 'this' improves cohesion. In the Conclusion what do these uses refer back to?**

'...and **this** is reducing shared family time'
a) What is reducing shared family time? _____

'A major change in social values is the key to changing **this** situation'.
b) What is the situation? _____

8   **Write your own essay conclusion in this box, in only two or three sentences.**

Activity 9   Write a complete essay

9   Now write your own essay. Spend no more than 40 minutes and write at least 250 words.

   Use the 5-paragraph structure, ensuring each body paragraph has a clear first (topic) sentence identifying the topic to be developed as those paragraphs are built.

   _____

   _____

When you have finished, compare your essay to the sample essay we have provided in the Treasure Chest.

 *Scan the QR code to access the **sample response for this essay** in the Treasure Chest or visit https://ielts-blog.com/treasure-chest*

IELTS Writing Task 2 Section

Boost Your Performance

Improvement starts with personal reflection! Review your most recent Task 2 writing and on this checklist tick those aspects on which you performed well. Those with no ticks indicate where work is still needed!

How did I do?

Good use of time

- ☐ Systematic routine
- ☐ No constant clock watching

Stick to the task

- ☐ Correct layout & appearance
- ☐ Your point of view in the intro paragraph
- ☐ Develop your position
- ☐ Systematic paragraph structure

Appropriate style and tone

- ☐ Formal tone
- ☐ Cautious language
- ☐ Formal vocabulary
- ☐ Appropriate use of idioms
- ☐ Use of connectors / referencing

Which aspects of Task 2 writing are proving difficult for you? Write a few of your thoughts down. Now read through the strategies below, and compare your own writing with our sample responses. Finally, rewrite your original Task 2 answers to build improvements.

If you had difficulties with any of the activities, read these strategies for guidance.

3 Key Strategies to Improve your Task 2 Writing

Strategy 1 - Good use of time

1. To use time well, follow a systematic routine when practising:

What you should do:	How?	Why?
Stage 1 — understand the task	By studying the wording and data for one to two minutes, especially the task type and central ideas	To guarantee relevance of your plan and clear structure of the answer and your viewpoint
Stage 2 — plan your answer for about two to three minutes	Build ideas linked to your own view and response type, establish paragraph structure	To organise your ideas into relevant paragraphs; to ensure clarity of answer
Stage 3 — write a systematic answer neatly and with clear paragraphing	By following your plan for about 30-35 minutes	To make your answer look organised, well structured, clear, and easier to read
Stage 4 — check your work quickly	By skim reading; quick word count by counting number of words in one line and then multiply by number of lines (e.g. 10 words x 25 lines = 250)	To pick up any obvious mistakes

Practise writing answers to Task 2 questions with a 40-minute limit. Follow the routine above, and gradually you will manage the restricted time, and will approach the task more professionally. It may also be useful to try one or two complete Writing tests within the official, one-hour, time limit so that you learn to combine the writing and time management patterns you have learnt for each task.

2. Don't become a 'clock victim'

Some candidates spend too much time counting words or watching the clock. They then lose focus and connection with the actual task. Practise writing Task 2 answers until you have developed a reliable routine.

Remember, if you are organised, you will create an organised answer. A relevant, organised answer seems professional to the assessor even if it still has some vocabulary and grammar weaknesses.

Strategy II - Stick to the task

1. Take care with the layout and appearance of your essay

A handwritten piece of writing, even a formal essay, is always a personal reflection of 'YOU' so you need to take particular care with its layout and appearance, even if you feel under time pressure. Avoid crossing out words too often and make your handwriting crisp and neat. Leave a line between each paragraph, so that the essay's structure is very clear.

2. Clarify your essay's viewpoint, direction and structure in the Introductory paragraph

In Western, academic essay writing, the Introduction often serves not just to introduce the topic but also to signal the writer's intentions or point of view (For example—whether you agree with the topic statement or not and what you are going to discuss).

If the assessor knows right at the beginning what your opinion and plan is, then this helps in three important ways:

a) It makes you appear well-organised (appearing to be a good essay manager is a good first impression).
b) It enables your reader (the assessor) to predict the likely direction of your essay—this helps the reading to go more smoothly (unless you don't do what you said you were going to do).
c) It forces you to be systematic and relevant in structuring the remainder of the essay.

3. Make sure you develop a clear point of view

Some candidates can write generally about the task topic but find it difficult to establish a clear point of view or a clear conclusion in terms of their own point of view. This is often related to a lack of experience in either thinking about or discussing social issues, or different cultural thinking styles.

The clearer your point of view is to your IELTS assessor the better the relationship between writer and reader is in this type of writing.

4. Use a systematic, paragraph structure

The use of clear paragraphs, each with a clear function or a clear central topic (idea) is one of the foundations of clear essay writing. It is a well-established convention in academic writing.

A well-organised and logically developed essay reduces 'scatter' of ideas (meaning, ideas, like a shopping list, written one after another without either links to previous ideas, development, or examples).

Strategy III - Appropriate style and tone

1. Establish an appropriate level of formality in your essay response

The use of language in any written communication reflects the relationship between writer and the context of writing (this means the situation in which the writing takes place and the expectations of the person who is to receive it).

You should try to build some of these features into your writing to create formality:

- Choose formal vocabulary mostly as this seems more professional to the reader.

- Avoid using clichés, short forms and abbreviations.

- Avoid repetition and over-use of basic verbs like 'is', 'has', 'makes', 'gets', 'does'.

- Vary your use of linking expressions.
  For instance, instead of writing 'For example' all the time, you can write, 'One example of this is....', or 'This is clearly illustrated in....'.

- Enrich your display of vocabulary by using adjectives or other expressions to create greater strength in your written 'voice', as in:
  'One effect of this is...' —> 'One striking effect of this is...';
  'This will lead to...'   —> 'Clearly, this will lead to...' ;
  'In contrast to this is...' —> 'In sharp contrast to this is....'.

- Reduce the use of personal pronouns where possible, by using 'it...' constructions, as in:
  'It seems reasonable to suggest that...' (instead of 'I think that...'), or
  'It is education that is the key to preventing extremism' (instead of 'I believe that education is the best way of stopping extremism').

- Use noun groups instead of lengthy imprecise formulations, as in:
  'There is currently an intensification of mature age unemployment' (rather than, 'Now there are many old workers and they don't have jobs and this is getting worse').

To summarise — your task is to try to match the assessor's expectations (as made explicit in the assessment criteria for Writing Tasks) as well as you can. Many readers today tend to read less formal English but are comfortable chatting in the language. When writing, this often limits vocabulary, reduces awareness of how to build and link ideas, and can lead to an inappropriately 'chatty' or repetitive essay.

2. Use modal forms or 'cautious language' to express views on complex issues

Even if your point of view is clear, social issues are complex and it is therefore difficult to be 100% certain about anything.

Example

Sentence 1

Family life **is** terrible today because work **is** full of stress and working hours **are** too long.

Sentence 2

For an increasing number of people family life nowadays **seems to be deteriorating**, perhaps, in part, because hours of work and levels of stress in many jobs **appear to be increasing.**

The assessor may think that Sentence 1 is too strong and simplistic because it is general and talks about family life as if it is 100% fact (use of '**is**' and '**are**' generally sound factual). Sentence 2 offers a more **cautious** formulation.

The tone of your writing forms part of the relationship with your reader. Tone in writing is similar to spoken voice tone. If you speak in a flat tone, you may appear bored or sad to the person you are speaking to; if your voice has a mix of high and low tones you sound more 'alive', more interesting. Similarly, if your written tone seems too sure and lacks caution when discussing complex social issues then your thinking may seem unreasonable or naïve, even if this is because of limited ability in English!

3. Use formal vocabulary to build range and give a more 'serious' tone to your essay

The writer of a high scoring Task 2 response is able to select vocabulary which indicates ability both to avoid repetition and demonstrate awareness of which words fit the topic and a formal type of essay writing in this context.

Example

Informal approach	Formal approach
Family life is really bad today	Family life seems to be deteriorating currently
People work too long	Working hours seem to be excessive
Jobs have a lot of stress	Some occupations seem to be generating increasing levels of stress
Something must be done about it	Action is required to tackle this problem
Government should stop all this or there'll be a really bad situation	The government needs to take preventive measures in order to avoid a social disaster
They should do something now	Immediate action seems important

Using a wider range of appropriate vocabulary flexibly, like a native speaker, strengthens the psychological connection that the assessor feels to your writing, even if there are still a few grammatical errors.

4. Use appropriate idioms occasionally to enrich vocabulary

Occasional idioms or less usual vocabulary extend the range and add to the 'colour' and 'personality' of your writing (so long as they are added sparingly and appropriately).

Example

Conversational style	Idiomatic alternative
The government must do something about this problem	The government must **grasp the nettle** in terms of this issue
Teenage kids and parents often get annoyed with each other	Parents and teenage children rarely **see things eye to eye**

It is better to avoid using common idioms in a forced way; they need to support your ideas naturally.

For example, avoid these over-used idioms or sayings:
- 'Every coin has two sides'
- 'To put it in a nutshell'
- 'Rome wasn't built in a day'

It's also not a good idea to:
- translate idioms from your own language into English, or
- use idioms unless you are really confident that they are currently used, and confident about precisely when and how they are used.

5. Use connectors and referencing pronouns to show relationship between your ideas

Ideas need to be connected using appropriate connecting expressions to help the reader follow the way you are building the explanations of your ideas and developing your point of view.

Example

Paragraph 1 - No connectors	Paragraph 2 - Good use of connectors
Marrying for money is rarely a good idea. Money leads to lack of feeling. People live in sadness. They are comfortable, of course. Being comfortable is not enough. People also need to feel loved.	Marrying for money is rarely a good idea **because this** may lead to a lack of feeling and **ultimately** the couple may live together in sadness, **even though** they are comfortable. **This type** of comfort is, **however**, not enough **since** people also need to feel loved.

The use of connecting expressions helps the reader and seems more mature. It also provides the reader with a better sense of your 'voice' as a writer.

Key Problems with Language in Writing Task 2

Think about the language you use when writing. What aspects of language are reducing the effectiveness of your responses?

How many of these 7 problems with language have you had in your recent Task 2 writing?

Language problems

Problem 1: Incorrect use of Word Forms (adjective/noun/adverb)

Problem 2: Inaccurate Verb Tenses

Problem 3: Lack of agreement between Subject and Verb

Problem 4: Poor use of Full Stops

Problem 5: Missing out important words

Problem 6: Careless Spelling

Problem 7: Repeating, repeating, repeating

 *Scan the QR code to download the **solutions for these problems** from the Treasure Chest or visit https://ielts-blog.com/treasure-chest*

WRITING CHECKPOINT TEST

IELTS Writing Section

Get Ready for the Checkpoint Test

You should by now have a better idea of yourself as an IELTS Test writer, and be more aware of the types of task you may need to respond to in your actual IELTS test, as well as some helpful strategies to boost your score.

Feeling confident?

If you feel confident, move straight on to the IELTS Writing Checkpoint test on the next page. Before you start, think about your profile as a writer - your strengths and weaknesses when taking this part of the test.

 *Scan the QR code to access a **blank answer sheet** in the Treasure Chest or visit https://ielts-blog.com/treasure-chest*

Feeling less confident?

If you are still struggling to master many of the aspects of written English expected in the IELTS Writing test, your best strategy is to go back and repeat the Entry test again.

Doing the Entry test again has several advantages:

- You will be familiar with what the Tasks require and can focus more easily on your actual writing
- You will be more relaxed and will understand better how to use the time more effectively
- You will remember your previous responses and know better how to improve and develop them

After repeating the Entry test, try to score yourself again. Was your writing better? In all four areas that are assessed or only in some? Review your weaknesses again, and then move on to the Checkpoint test.

IELTS WRITING CHECKPOINT TEST

TASK 1

You should spend about 20 minutes on this task.

The two diagrams below describe changes to a museum's floor plan between 2008 and 2012.

Summarise the information by selecting and reporting the key features, and make any relevant comparisons.

Write at least 150 words.

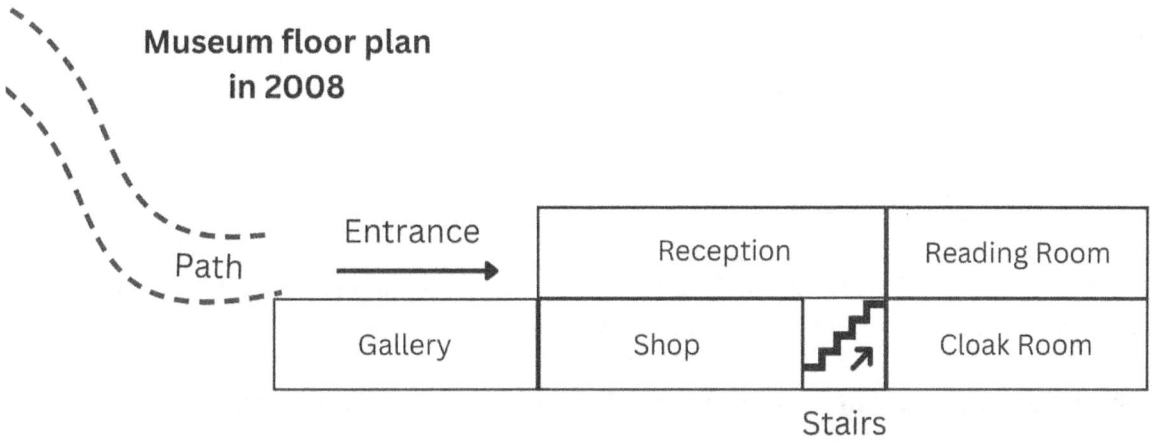

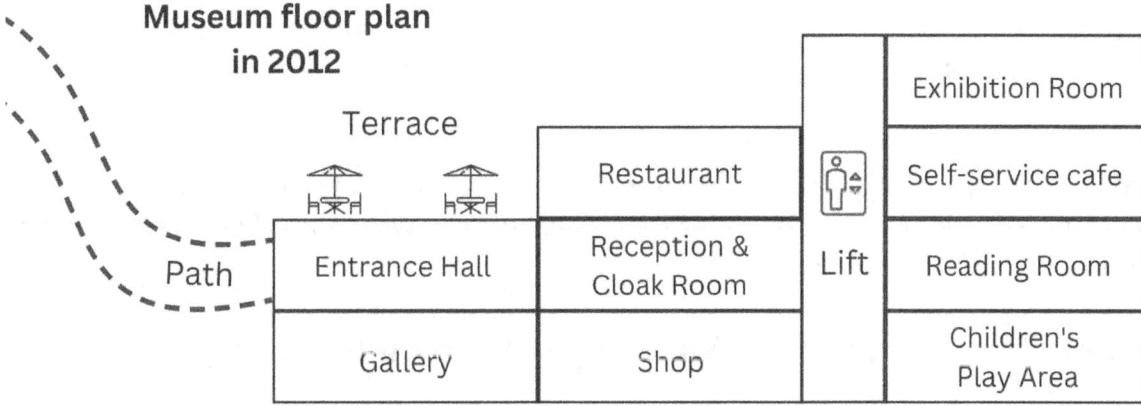

IELTS Writing Section

TASK 2

You should spend about 40 minutes on this task.

Write about the following topic:

> In the past older people spent time with others and exercised daily. Nowadays many of them suffer from loneliness and health problems. What are the reasons for this? What can be done to improve the situation?
>
> Give reasons for your answer and include any relevant ideas from your own knowledge or experience.

Write at least 250 words.

Finished the Checkpoint test?

Do a self-assessment of your Writing for the Checkpoint test, using the assessment criteria used for the Entry test on pages 99-100. Again, compare your writing with the sample responses.

> The sample responses are located in the IELTS Answers section at the end of this book.

Repeat the review process to build further awareness of your ongoing weaknesses, and to chart where your test techniques and writing skills have improved. Repeat the Checkpoint test a few days later.

At the end of this book there will be a final test for you to try (Exit test) but this time you should take all four parts of the IELTS test at the same sitting (Listening, Reading, Writing and Speaking), and then award scores for all parts of the Exit test.

Now, it's time to move on to the Speaking section on the next page.

SPEAKING ENTRY TEST

IELTS Speaking Section

Get Ready

In the IELTS Speaking test you will be interviewed and given a score by a trained IELTS assessor. After the assessor has checked your identity, **the interview is in 3 parts:**

Part 1 - general questions about yourself and daily life (3-4 minutes)

Part 2 - a short talk for up to 2 minutes on a topic provided (plus one minute to prepare)

Part 3 - more extended questions linked to the topic of the talk (3-4 minutes)

The assessor will award you a score from 0-9 based on your performance.

How to respond well in the IELTS interview

- Be polite and be aware of the timing of the interview parts.
- Use a good variety of language and avoid too much repetition, if you can.
- If you don't understand a question, ask for it to be repeated using different words.
- Try to answer with good intonation so that your responses sound interesting.

 **It will be really helpful if you can record your Speaking Entry Test as it happens, to have a better opportunity to score, review, and compare your performance with that of another student.**

 Scan the QR code to access the **Speaking Entry Test recording** *in the Treasure Chest or visit https://ielts-blog.com/treasure-chest*

Are you ready? Start the Entry Test now.

IELTS SPEAKING ENTRY TEST

Test Instructions

1. Listen to the **Introduction** and **Part 1** and respond to each question. **Pause** the recording before answering each question.

2. After the introduction to Part 2, **pause** the recording for **one minute** to make notes.

3. After the one minute, **start** the recording again. After you hear, 'Could you start talking now, please', **pause** the recording again and start talking for a minimum of one and a maximum of two minutes.

4. **Start** the recording again after two minutes maximum, listen to and answer the rounding off question. Then just **continue** as the interview moves into **Part 3**.

5. **Pause** the recording before answering each question in Part 3.

Test Questions

PART 1

Let's talk about what you do

- Are you studying or do you have a job?
- What do you enjoy most about your course / job?
- What range of subjects do you have to study on your course / job?
- Do you think you made the right choice of course / job?
- What will you do after your course / job has finished?

NOTE If you are not studying a course currently, answer the questions about a previous course, or about your current job

I'd like to talk about shopping now.

- How often do you go shopping?
- What things do you most enjoy buying?
- Do you ever shop online?
- Is shopping a good way to spend your leisure time?

I'd like to consider talking with friends now

- How often do you talk to your friends?
- What do you usually talk about?
- Is text messaging a good way to talk to friends?
- Do you prefer talking to family or to friends?

PART 2

> **Talk about someone in your family who is really kind. You should say**
>
> - who this person is
> - what their background is
> - what acts of kindness they do
>
> and explain why you think this person is so kind

Rounding-off question: Are you a kind person?

PART 3

You've been talking about someone in your family who is really kind and I'd like to discuss with you a few more questions related to the same topic.

Let's consider first of all kindness and families.

- Describe some ways in which parents in your country teach their children to be kind to others.
- Are women in families generally kinder than men, do you think?

Let's move on now to discuss kindness and feelings.

- Can you be a happy person if you are not also a kind person?
- Do you think it's easier to be kind to others or to be critical of others?

Let's talk briefly about the topic of kindness in society

- Are governments showing less and less concern for poor people in their societies, do you think?
- Should children do community work, do you think, by helping poor or sick people as a compulsory part of their school studies?

That is the end of the Entry Speaking test.

Score, Review then Practise

Score your Entry Test

Now you have finished the Entry Test, listen to the responses of another test taker to the same interview, and compare them with your own.

 *Scan the QR code to access the **recording of Sabeen's Speaking Test** in the Treasure Chest or visit https://ielts-blog.com/treasure-chest*

The approximate scores Sabeen would get in IELTS are listed in the table below. Using them as a guide, give yourself a score for your own responses in the table below. Remember, the IELTS band scale goes from 0 - 9.

Of course, it will be very difficult for you to give yourself an accurate score but don't worry if the scores you award yourself are either too high or too low. The aim here is to build your awareness both of how scores are awarded, and how your performance compares with that of another test taker.

Add the four individual scores together and divide your total score by 4 for an approximate overall band score for your interview.

Assessment Criteria	What it means	Your score (0-9)	Sabeen's score (0-9)
Fluency and Coherence (FC)	A high score means the test taker can keep speaking without much hesitation, pausing between words or self-correction. Their answers should be appropriate and well-developed and their ideas organised and connected using a range of linking words.		6
Lexical Resource (LR)	A high score means the test taker can convey their thoughts clearly using a good variety of appropriate words and expressions, as well as paraphrasing particular words or phrases they can't remember while talking.		6
Grammatical Range and Accuracy (GRA)	A high score means the test taker's sentences are mostly grammatically correct and they are able to use complex as well as simple sentences.		6
Pronunciation (Pron)	A high score means the listener can understand the test taker easily. This includes correct pronunciation, intonation (raising and lowering the voice appropriately) and the use of chunking - organising your sentences into small, manageable spoken units and pauses between them.		7
Total Score	(FC + LR + GRA + Pron) / 4		6

Review

Once you have decided your own scores on all four criteria for your interview, check the Treasure Chest for our detailed "Analysis and Scores for Sabeen" to understand how IELTS Speaking is marked and what affects the score in each assessment criterion. Then read "How could Sabeen have done better?" to understand what can be done to improve each score.

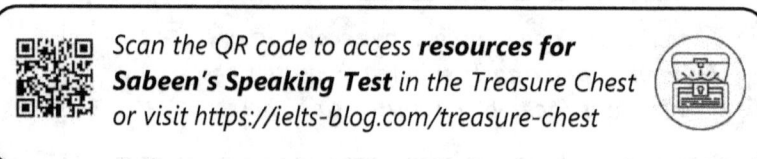

Now go back to your responses and either listen to them or review them again in detail, with a focus on one assessment criterion at a time.

Try to identify the main weaknesses in your interview. Here are a few questions to guide you:

- Did I seem relaxed and able to talk without too much hesitation?
- Were my responses clear and well-constructed without too much repetition?
- Was my grammar accurate - verb tenses, verb agreement, pronouns, for example?
- Did I use a good variety of vocabulary, with some higher-level words, not just simple ones?
- Did my responses sound interesting because of good intonation?
- Did I talk for long enough during the talk, and develop and extend my responses in the final part?

Answering questions like these will help you to get a better idea of your abilities in the interview.

Practise

Once your review has helped you to get a much better idea of your strengths and weaknesses as a speaker, either repeat the Entry Speaking Test, or, move on to the next section of this book and practise more question types and response language. Focus especially on areas that are still difficult for you. Check, too, the useful strategies given, and ways to solve common test-taking problems.

Boost Your Performance

For any speaking activities that you still find troublesome, check the useful test strategies given and ways to solve common test-taking problems. Then try those challenging speaking activities again, and change any of your answers that seem weak.

SPEAKING TEST PRACTICE

WHAT'S INSIDE:

- Activities to Prepare You for the Test
- Boost Your Performance

Activities to Prepare You for the Test

PART 1 Answering questions on some everyday topics

It is natural at the start of the interview to feel nervous and unsure. The interviewer will start by asking one or two questions to check your identity.

The best strategy in Part 1 is to answer questions on each everyday topic in a friendly and relaxed way. This will help to release your English, and build your confidence.

Complete Activities 1-16 for a better understanding of Speaking Part 1.

The activities in this section will explore some differences between stronger and weaker responses, to improve your own responses when you try the IELTS Practice Test.

 The answers are located in the IELTS Answers section at the end of this book.

Activities 1 - 5   Build stronger responses to the Warm-Up questions

Warm Up	Questions to get to know you

1   Question: 'Do you live in an apartment or a house?'

   Which of these possible responses seems the most appropriate, and why?

   a) A house.
   b) I live in a house in West Beach; I've lived there for about 2 years now.
   c) I live in a house. The house is big.

2   Question: 'Is it a good place to live? (Why?/Why not?)'

   Which response is not really answering what the question is asking?

   a) Yes, it's the suburb that is near the city centre, with all the best shops.
   b) Not really, as it's located in a very noisy part of town and the landlord never does anything about our complaints.
   c) Yes it's a really good place because the rent is reasonable and it's near to the train station.

IELTS Speaking Section

3 Question: 'Is the area where you live pleasant? (Why?/Why not?)'

Which response is a good one? What seems wrong with each of the other two?

a) It's pleasant, yes. It's pleasant because it has very pleasant parks nearby. These parks are nice and big, with nice flowers, and nice trees.

b) Yes, it's great. There are plenty of parks, with tennis courts, and many varied, native plants, flowers and trees. Also the houses are all well-built and up-to-date.

c) Yes it has...er...it has pleasant surroundings...er...and very attractive parks, with sports... erm... facilities... and...very little... erm poll...pollu...pollution.

4 Question: 'What facilities are there near your home?'

Which seems the best way to ask for this question to be repeated?

a) I'm sorry I didn't catch that. Could you repeat it please?
b) I don't understand. Can you say it again?
c) What are 'facilities', please? I need to hear the question again.

5 Which response to the Warm Up question in activity 4 seems the clearest?

a) There are facilities, yes, there are a park, I go sometimes, a sports ground for I think for soccer. Kids go there, from street where I live.

b) There are lots – a park, for example, which I go to sometimes, and a sports ground, for soccer, I think. Some of the kids from my street go there.

c) Near my home are lots facilities, like there is a park for me to go there and a soccer sports ground for street kids from where I live in.

Activities 6 - 9   Build stronger responses to questions on Topic 1

Topic 1   Let's move on to talk about friends

6 Question: 'Do you have many friends or just one or two?'

Complete this response using the expressions in the box below.

I have _____ of friends... some from right back when I was at school, others from various jobs I've had, and there are the friends I play _____ with. I've always been a _____ sort of person so I find it easy to _____ on with people when I _____ them. But, I _____ I'd say I only have one or two _____ friends – friends I completely trust, I _____.

suppose	mean	true	meet	sport	friendly	get	loads

IELTS Speaking Section

7 **Question: 'How often do you see your friends?'**

Which response has some high-level vocabulary and idioms in it?

a) I don't have much chance to catch up with my old friends at the moment, as I'm studying here in Australia and they're not, but I often bump into my new friends at college here, and we hang out together.

b) Most of my old friends are back at home, and I'm here in Australia. I have lots of new friends from college and we like to meet up and do things...all sorts of things together. It's good.

c) Wow...Let me see...I don't see my school friends much...as they're at home and I'm not...if you know what I mean...so I don't see them often...but my new Aussie, college friends...well, of course, I see them all the time...too much maybe!

8 **Question: 'Are you good at making new friends? (Why?/Why not?)'**

Which response (a-c) is the most grammatically accurate?

a) As I say, I'm pretty good at make friend because I'm easygoing and I like meet new people when I'm going out to parties or thing like that.

b) As I'm saying, I like people so it's easier making friends. I'm good at chatting, you say 'small talk' I think. People seem like me maybe because I laugh much.

c) As I said just before, I'm a bit shy but I make friends quite easily, maybe because I'm a good listener, and I like asking questions and showing interest in people.

9 **Question: 'Which are more important – friends or family (Why?)'**

Which response (a-c) seems the most interesting and varied?

a) I think family is more important, because everyone has a family. Friends sometimes don't last but your family is with you for ever. You always have a family – parents, brothers, sisters and if you're lucky, your grandparents, of course. It's normal to have a lot of family around you.

b) Family definitely. They are with you and care for you from the beginning of your life, they shape the person you become, they always support you and love you unconditionally. They will always be there if you get into difficulties. Friends don't always feel the same level of responsibility.

c) Both are important, but family is more important. I really love my mother, and she loves me. It's natural I suppose but it's important to me, and to her. My friends like me and I like them but it's not the same really. It's a different feeling, less important really, at least for me.

Activities 10 - 13   Build stronger responses to questions on Topic 2:

Topic 2	Let's talk now about cars and driving

10   Question: 'Can you drive? (Why?/Why not?)'

Which response (a-c) uses the most advanced and varied linking expressions?

a) I can't drive at the moment; however, I'd like to learn because it will be useful, even though I don't need to drive as part of my job, as I work in an office.'

b) I can drive, yes. I learnt last year and I have a small car, but I don't drive very often. Petrol is much too expensive for me and I'm only a student.

c) I've been driving for ten years. In my country it is not easy to learn to drive because lessons are so expensive so it cost me about $800 to get my licence.

11   Question: 'Is traffic increasing on roads in your country?'

Which response (a-c) seems the most relevant?

a) There are many cars on our roads, especially taxis. The roads never seem to be quiet, and it's always so noisy and there is a lot of pollution. It's not really safe to drive these days.

b) The roads are increasing but we need more because the population is increasing very rapidly too. Everyone wants a car and luckily, we make our own cars now and they are quite cheap.

c) It's increasing rapidly, yes. This is mainly because more people can now afford to buy cars, and so the increasing levels of traffic are very noticeable – more traffic jams, and more accidents.

12   Question: 'How can car accidents be stopped?'

Which response (a-c) seems too direct and possibly impolite?

a) It's probably unlikely that car accidents can be stopped completely. Life is often too hectic, so people have more difficulty concentrating and the roads are busier. All these factors put ever greater pressure on drivers, I think.'

b) They can't. It's not possible. Think about it. Can you drive and answer your mobile phone and remember what you need to buy from the shops, and talk to the children in the back seat. Nor me. That's why there are accidents.

c) It's not possible, really. If you think about it, many drivers have a lot of stress when they drive – stress from other people in the car, mobile phones, time pressure. Put all these together and it's not surprising that accidents happen.

IELTS Speaking Section

13   Question: 'How do you feel when you are in a car that is going very fast?'

In which response (a-c) is hesitation managed most successfully?

a) I feel...erm I feel scare...scared because I don't always...I don't trust the driving...sorry the driver. If I know the driver...and I know the driver drives...erm, safer, I mean safely, then I could...can relax a little bit

b) I feel...scare...sorry I meant to say, I feel scared, because I don't always...how can I put it, I don't always trust the driving, I mean driver. If I know the driver...erm or more important, if I know the driver drives...safer, or rather, safely, then I could...or can relax a little bit

c) I feel...I feel scare...scared because I don't always...I don't trust the driving...the driver. If I know the driver...and I know the driver drives...safer, sorry, safely, then I could...I'm sorry, can relax a little bit.

Activities 14 - 16   Improve your pronunciation skills

14   Building Awareness of 'Chunking'

Good speakers group words into 'chunks', which are units of meaning separated by little pauses. This helps the listener to absorb information more easily. The pauses are only short to retain fluency and avoid being mistaken for hesitation.

Example

Compare A with B:
A   IcomefromTehranit'sareallybusycitywithmanymarketsandmosques
B   I come from Tehran • It's a really busy city • with many markets and mosques

Now try to 'chunk' the following responses from Part 1 in a similar way

I'msorryIdidn'tcatchthatCouldyourepeatitplease?

Yesit'sgreatTherearplentyofparkswithtenniscourtsandmanynative plantsflowersandtrees.

AsIsaidjustbeforeI'mabitshybutImakefriendsquiteeasilymaybebecauseI'ma goodlistenerandIlikeaskingquestionsandshowinginterestinpeople.

Finally, practise saying each sentence in 'chunks', using only very short pauses.

15 Building Awareness of Stress and Rhythm

English is a stress-timed language, and follows a pattern a bit like a drumbeat, so some words or sounds are spoken more loudly (stressed) and others are spoken more quickly and softly in a fairly regular time. This establishes rhythm.

Example

Let's imagine you want to say this sentence:

'I went for a meal last night but the waiter forgot my order'.

To apply stress and create rhythm you would need to say it a little like this:

I wENt for a MEal last nIGHt • but the WAIter forGOT my ORder

What is happening in this version of the sentence? Let's analyse it:

- Only part of each stressed word receives the strongest sound **(MAIN STRESS)**
- Some words also have some stress but it is less strong (e.g. last, but, my)
- The end of a stressed word may become weakly pronounced in order not to disturb the rhythm (e.g. the 't' sound in 'went' and 'night' may hardly be heard)
- All the unstressed parts (highlighted, e.g. t for a, al last n) are spoken at a faster speed, and each occupies about the same time length, to maintain a spoken rhythm.
- The listener 'catches' the information because it is the information-carrying words that are stressed (**went, meal, night, waiter, forgot, order**)

Analyse these spoken responses from Part 1, using the style in the Example

a) It's normal to have a lot of family around you.

_____

b) ...so the increasing levels of traffic are very noticeable.

_____

c) It's probably unlikely that car accidents can be stopped completely.

_____

d) ...I'm a good listener, and I like asking questions and showing interest in people.

_____

Say each sentence aloud. Try to build the stress 'drumbeat', and the rhythm it creates.

IELTS Speaking Section

16 Building Awareness of Intonation

Intonation is like the 'song' of a language – it helps you to express feelings and personality. Some languages invite more variety of 'song' than others. When you speak English, it really helps to develop a good range of tones (from high to low) because:

- it adds interest to your voice and to the meanings and feelings you are expressing
- it makes the listener feel more focused and more connected to you as a person

Intonation is helpful in IELTS when you are expressing something you have real feelings about.

Example

Assessor: Do you like driving?

Speaker A: I **LOVE** it • it's my **TO**tal **PASS**ion • I feel compl**ETE**ly al**IVe** when I **DRI**ve.

Speaker B: L O VE   T O tal P A S S ion   E T E ly al IVE
                 I   it • it's my   • I feel compl   when I **DRI**ve.

Speaker B lifts the tone on some of the stressed words and also says them a little more slowly at the same time to show how much feeling is involved.

Study these responses. Identify parts where 'feelings' invite a higher tone, and a slower delivery.

a) I really love my family, especially my grandmother; she's such a beautiful person.

_____

b) I make friends really easily; in fact I get super excited when I meet new people.

_____

c) I'm a terrible driver. I get totally nervous in heavy traffic, and when I get out of the car I feel like a total wreck! I'm so annoyed with myself about it!

_____

Practise saying these responses in a way which communicates the feelings.

IELTS Speaking Section

Now it's your turn to practise speaking!

Listen to the questions on the recording and practise answering as if you were in a real IELTS interview.

 *Scan the QR code to access the **Speaking Part 1 recording** in the Treasure Chest or visit https://ielts-blog.com/treasure-chest*

 If possible, record your answers for later analysis. For example, you could analyse how long your responses were, how varied, fluent, grammatical, and interesting. This is part of learning about, and managing your spoken performance.

PART 2   Giving a short talk on a topic

In this part, the assessor gives you a topic card. On it is guidance on what aspects of the topic to talk about. You have one minute to prepare before you talk.

The best strategy is to use the planning time to note down ideas for each of the areas mentioned on the card. This will structure your talk and give you confidence.

Complete Activities 1-7 for a better understanding of Speaking Part 2.

The activities in this section will help you train yourself to prepare effectively for the talk and deliver a relevant and coherent speech.

   The answers are located in the IELTS Answers section at the end of this book.

Activities 1 - 7   Build a stronger response to the Topic Card question

Task Card: An interesting life

> Talk about someone you know, or know about, who has had an interesting life. You should say:
>
> - who the person is
> - where the person comes from
> - what is interesting about that person's life
>
> and say why that person's life seems interesting to you

1   Choose either a), b) or c). To practise building ideas, list four interesting things about their life:

Person \ Interesting things	1	2	3	4
a) Someone you know well				
b) A famous person				
c) Yourself				

IELTS Speaking Section

2 Imagine someone received the task card above and has chosen to talk about their brother.

Task Card	Notes (a-k)
1) Who the person is	_____
2) Where the person comes from	_____
3) What is interesting about that person's life	_____
4) and say why that person's life seems interesting to you	_____

Match the notes (a-k), about the candidate's brother, with the 4 parts of the task card.

Notes

a) my brother, Pierre b) born deaf c) brilliant scholar
d) 5 years' older than me e) now lives New Zealand f) took risks, unlike me
g) born Paris h) now an artist i) sailed solo to NZ
j) met his wife in NZ k) never allowed disability to spoil his life

3 Which beginning to the talk (a-c) seems the most appropriate to you, and why?

a) My brother is interesting. His name is Pierre. He is five years' older than me so I'm the younger one. He comes from Paris originally but now he is in New Zealand

b) All right. Well, I suppose all lives are fascinating in some ways, but I'd like to talk briefly about my brother, Pierre. His life has been really extraordinary, at least in my opinion. Let me explain.

c) Pierre is my brother. He's my older brother in fact – five years older. He has had an interesting life, for sure, very interesting. Mine has been not so interesting. He was born in Paris, in fact we both were born there.

4 Sometimes candidates have trouble talking for two minutes, for different reasons.

Which two of these candidates (a-c) are having trouble and for what reasons?

a) My brother Pierre, is from Paris. He is interesting because he is deaf. He has done many things – he was good at school, he was an artist, he sailed to New Zealand on his own and got married there. Why is he interesting? Because he never let disability spoil his life, he took risks, not like me.

b) We born...were born...in France...in Paris. His name, my brother's name...is Pierre...and he is five years' more...five years' old...five years' older...of...I mean, than I...me. So...she is...his...he is my grand...big brother...and my...I am a...baby...the baby for...of the family.

c) My brother, Pierre, in fact he's my older brother, as there's five years' difference in our ages, was born in Paris, actually very close to the centre of Paris, where our parents had a very popular local bakery. Although he was born deaf, Pierre was brilliant at school, especially at mathematics and Art...

5   The task card may finally ask you, Why…? so answer with reasons, not just information.

Which of (a-c) does this best?

a) Why my brother is interesting? He is interesting because he has done all those things —sailing, art, moving to a new country. He has done more things than me. I didn't travel much and don't take many risks, like he does. I tend to stay at home.

b) My brother has always seemed especially interesting to me because he was born deaf and this created distance between us. As a younger brother I wanted to look up to him, but it was not easy as his disability made him seem so different. But he inspired me because he never let his deafness stop him from taking risks, or from seeking adventure.

c) His life is interesting. It is not easy to be a deaf boy and he has still managed to do lots of things, often things that are risky. Sailing to New Zealand was risky but he did it, and he did it alone. It took him nine months, but he finally got there to New Zealand. We met him there…the whole family met him.

6   If you stop after only one minute, the assessor may invite you to say more, so try to expand your talk. After that, you can signal that you have finished.

Which way of ending your talk (a-c) seems the most appropriate and polite?

a) I finish now.
b) That's it, no more to say. I said it all.
c) I think that's all I have to say on this topic, for now, anyway.

7   After the talk, a 'rounding off' question may be asked. Give a brief, interesting answer.

Which answer (a-c) seems the most appropriate?

Assessor: Do you see your brother very often?

a) No, not really. I live in Paris still and he's in New Zealand. It's a long journey to go from France to there, or even the other way…it takes a long time, too long for me.

b) No, not often. He doesn't make contact very often…he's busy. I think he's too busy to make regular contact. I'm quite usually busy too most of the time, I must say.

c) Not as often as I'd like. He came over to Paris last year for our parents' 30th wedding anniversary but flights are a bit too expensive for us to get together regularly.

IELTS Speaking Section

Now it's your turn to practise speaking!

Listen to the question on the recording and practise answering as if you were in a real IELTS interview.

 *Scan the QR code to access the **Speaking Part 2 recording** in the Treasure Chest or visit https://ielts-blog.com/treasure-chest*

1. After the introduction to Part 2, **pause** the recording for **one minute** to make notes. Here is the task card:

> **Talk about a time when you were a child and got into trouble. You should say:**
> - how old you were
> - what you did that got you into trouble
> - what happened afterwards
>
> **and say why you still remember this occasion.**

2. After the one minute, **start** the recording again. After you hear, 'Could you start talking now, please', **pause** the recording again and start talking.

3. Start the recording again after **two minutes** and listen to the rounding off question.

4. Answer the question.

 If possible, record your answers for later analysis. For example, you could analyse how long your responses were, how varied, fluent, grammatical, and interesting. This is part of learning about, and managing your spoken performance.

IELTS Speaking Section

PART 3   Answering questions on the talk topic

In this final part, the assessor asks questions related to the Part 2 talk topic.

The best strategy is to use your answers to show your English at a higher level by adding greater variety of vocabulary and good linking language. This is your chance to show the assessor that you have a good range of spoken ability and can discuss ideas maturely. It will help to leave the assessor with a positive overall impression of your level.

Complete Activities 1-5 for a better understanding of Speaking Part 3.

The activities in this section explore differences between stronger and weaker responses to help improve your own responses when you try the IELTS Practice Test.

 The answers are located in the IELTS Answers section at the end of this book.

Activities 1 - 5   Build a stronger response to questions in Part 3

1   Which response (a-c) to the first question, extends the topic fully and relevantly?

Assessor: Let's talk about exciting activities. Can you tell me about some exciting leisure activities in your culture?

a) There are many exciting activities in my country. You can do sports, of course, like soccer, and basketball, or you can do more exciting activities like mountain climbing or skiing. It all depends on your interest and your money, of course. Some of these sports cost a lot of money so not everyone can do them. I wasn't able to do such things as a child.

b) It's true that these days people are more interested in exciting activities, even dangerous ones, In my country skydiving has become popular, and also hunting for wild boar. Hunting is dangerous because it is unpredictable, partly because the boars are aggressive and can run very fast. This mix of danger and excitement seems increasingly attractive, at least to some people.

c) I think it all depends on what you think is exciting. I'm not a very brave person so many things are exciting for me. Some of my friends, however, love excitement and like to do more interesting things. If I go for a picnic in the mountains, this is really exciting for me, not the food of course, but the steep places and the views.

2   Occasionally the assessor may respond to your answer with a rounding off question.

Which response (a-c) seems the most relaxed and natural?

Assessor: Why don't you like dangerous activities?

a) I don't know. I don't like them. They seem rather stupid to me. I never liked to do dangerous activities when I was younger, and I'm the same now. I like an easy life not a difficult life. In a nutshell, I like to stay in the land of living.

b) Why do you think I don't like dangerous activities? I like some. I like skiing for example. That's dangerous sometimes. Some people get killed from skiing accidents, but I never think of that. I like this sport too much.

c) Well, maybe I'm just a bit of a coward, though I don't think so. I like to think I'm just sensible, that's all. Everyone has to decide what they can or can't do, and so I just try to be careful. I don't think I'm alone, I'm sure many people are like that.

3   The next question might ask you to imagine the situation in the future.

Which response (a-c) has the greatest variety of grammar?

Assessor: Do you think in the future people will choose to lead more dangerous lives?

a) Yes, I do for sure. I think people will try to do very unusual things like space trips or they will go on endurance walks in dangerous places with no guide or maybe they will even sleep in haunted houses or shoot rapids on a log.

b) Yes, more and more dangerous, you're right. It is part of life. People always want to go beyond their limits and other people are happy to take their money and to organise some new dangerous activity, like shark hunting.

c) It seems likely that this trend will continue, yes. This is probably because people psychologically seek danger even though they know it's risky. However high the risk, there are always people who are willing to have a go.

4 When the assessor moves on to more complex topics, it's your chance to discuss ideas in depth, using greater variety of language.

Which response (a-c) has the richest vocabulary? Circle the high-level vocabulary in it.

Assessor: Let's talk now about the best ways to build your life. Can you explain why nowadays more young people wait until they are older before they get married?

a) I suppose there may be a whole host of reasons, but generally speaking, I think the pressure of building a career is stronger now. In fact, sometimes young graduates struggle to find permanent jobs and if they have a succession of temporary positions, they probably don't feel financially secure enough to face the responsibility of marriage. Also, most marriages depend on both partners having the potential to earn good salaries, so for many women a career is built first, and marriage and family is put off until later.

b) I think there are many reasons but many people need a career today and it is very difficult to find a good job, even if you have been to university. Some people have one temporary job after another and don't think they have enough money to get married. Today husband and wife often both have jobs, and actually both need jobs. Many women try to have a good job before they think about getting married and having children. They will probably work again too even when their children are young.

c) You have to have a good job these days, it's very important, because it's hard to find a really good job - I mean a job that is not part-time or just for a few months. So, without a real job and a good salary many men and many women don't have the confidence to get married, and to have children, especially as children are expensive too! This is a problem for many women, I think, who know they must probably work and have children, so they try to get a good job first and they marry later, have children and then try to work part-time.

5 Part 3 may only last around 4 minutes if the assessor is, by then, confident of your level, so answer the questions with maximum range and variety.

Circle the linking words (e.g. however, whereas) in the reply (a-c) that uses them best.

Assessor: Do you think your life has been more interesting than your parents' lives?

a) I don't think it is easy to answer this question. I have certainly travelled more than my parents but it's not easy to say my experiences have been more interesting. My parents had a simple life when they were young but it was rich in its own way. They had more regular contact with members of their extended family – erm cousins, aunts, uncles, and grandparents. I have to say I don't even know some of my cousins as they live in other countries, and are dotted all over the world. Perhaps my life has been less interesting in terms of contact with wider family. Their family life was richer, for sure.

b) To be honest, I can't really say. Even though I think I've had more opportunities to travel than may parents did, it's not very easy to compare different experiences in terms of level of interest. While my parents' early life was simple, it did have its own richness. Compared to my upbringing, for instance, theirs involved more regular contact with family members. For example, they spent more time with cousins, aunts, uncles, and grandparents, whereas I haven't met some of my cousins, simply because they live in other countries. So, from that point of view, my life has probably been less interesting than theirs.

c) This is an interesting question. I don't think interest can be compared...it's very personal. OK I know I have travelled more than my parents did. It was interesting for me but different from their early life. My parents' early life tended to be simple but to them I'm sure it was really interesting. I know they had a lot more contact with family members like cousins, aunts and uncles and grandparents than I've had. In fact, I don't know many of my cousins and have never even met them. They live all over the world in different countries. So, my parents' family life was definitely more interesting than mine, I believe.

Now it's your turn to practise speaking!

Listen to the recording and practise answering as if you were in a real IELTS interview.

 *Scan the QR code to access the **Speaking Part 3 recording** in the Treasure Chest or visit https://ielts-blog.com/treasure-chest*

 If possible, record your answers and listen to them. It's good practice to re-record your own responses, each time trying to improve some aspect of your language – pronunciation, grammar, vocabulary, fluency and coherence.

IELTS Speaking Section

Boost Your Performance

Improvement starts with personal reflection! Review the most recent version of your Practice Speaking Test answers and, on this checklist, tick those aspects on which you performed well. Those with no ticks indicate where work is still needed!

How did I do?

First impressions

- ☐ My opinions weren't too strong or controversial
- ☐ I used genuine personal experience

Use of language

- ☐ My answers related directly to the questions (not off-topic)
- ☐ I extended responses with examples
- ☐ I used accurate grammar
- ☐ My vocabulary use was varied
- ☐ I used suitable idioms <u>occasionally</u>

Pronunciation

- ☐ Chunking
- ☐ Correct sentence stress and rhythm
- ☐ Correct intonation ('voice music')

Rerecord your answers to the questions with a particular focus on the issues you identified using the checklist above. Then compare your second attempt to your original to judge improvements.

If you had difficulties with any of the activities, read these strategies for guidance.

Strategy 1 - Create a positive impression

1. Dress smartly and tidily but not too formally

Dress choices often reflect one's culture. Dressing too formally might suggest trying to influence the assessor positively, so just dress smartly and tidily in order to feel relaxed and comfortable.

2. Be truthful in your answers

Truthfulness is not being assessed, but you will feel more comfortable representing yourself honestly. With any question or topic that is outside your own experience try talking about a relative or friend as an example. There is no penalty for this, as it is only your language that is being assessed.

3. Be friendly, but take the test seriously

Some assessors may seem more formal than others. Their complex job is to be as fair as possible so be cooperative and helpful. Chatting too much or being over-friendly with the assessor does not suit a first meeting. Find the 'middle way' - friendlier and less formal for the general questions in Part 1; a little more formal in Part 3, when discussing issues and giving your opinions.

4. Don't worry too much about saying the wrong thing, but...

It is a good strategy not to say things that are too strong, too controversial or too personal in case the assessor who disagrees with your views is affected unconsciously.

Strategy II - Connect with your assessor

1. Treat the assessor as an equal, not as a 'boss'

In western cultures confidence and being positive produce energy and reduce any 'power gap' between two people.

2. Make eye contact appropriately

In western cultural terms, eye contact demonstrates personal connection and makes the assessor feel comfortable as she often has to look down to read the questions.

3. Respond to comments the assessor makes

Occasionally the assessor may comment on something you say. It builds a better connection if you respond. **Example:**

Assessor: It sounds as though you don't really trust the idea of marriage.

You: ***Does it? Maybe you're right.*** *I think it's definitely true that marriage seems more risky these days, as in this type of society people are more selfish, more independent and less respectful of tradition and so they may not feel so deeply connected to any promises they make.*

4. Don't 'fish' for feedback at the end of the test

If you ask, 'How did I do?' at the end of the test you will receive no feedback. The assessor cannot discuss the result or your performance. Just say something polite as you leave the room.

5. Use your personal experiences

Speaking about your own life generates examples and comparisons, thus extending answers, and forming a stronger connection with the assessor. People in English-speaking cultures often view this positively.

6. Cooperate with the assessor's time considerations

The assessor has a strict time schedule to cover the three parts of the interview. Help the assessor by pacing your answers to the 'rhythm' of each part of the interview, thus avoiding tricky adjustments.

Strategy III - Demonstrate good use of language

1. Take care when building answers

The assessor judges whether or not your answers are coherent. This means whether your ideas are linked together and easy to follow. **Linking ideas makes you a good communicator** because you are helping the listener as much as you can.

Example: *I like pets **because** pets are friends. People have pets **so that** they are less lonely.*

2. Extend your responses - say it, explain it, support it

Beginning responses in a structured and organised way, especially in Part 3, both extends, and adds coherence to them. Chances arise for more varied sentence types and vocabulary.

Assessor: Do you think weddings are a good idea these days?

Your response:

Say it:	*Well not really, in fact I suppose I'm a bit anti-weddings.*
Explain it:	*By saying this I suppose I mean that at many weddings today there seems, to my mind at least, to be too much emphasis on display and perhaps not enough attention given to deep meaning.*
Support it:	*For example, I've seen many of my friends' marriages fail and this has made me a little pessimistic about expensive, 'showy' wedding ceremonies that seem mainly about displays of wealth. It's the deep commitment of two people that is the core of a marriage.*

3. Don't drift off-topic

It's important to make your answers fit the questions asked, and for your ideas to connect together clearly. Study this example. **Response 1** is less relevant to the question about marriage in general; **Response 2** is more relevant.

Assessor: What do you imagine will happen to marriage in the future?

Response 1: I'm not sure if I'll get married in the future. I want to get a good job and build my career so that I don't have to worry too much about money. Maybe I'll think about getting married after that.

Response 2: I think marriage will become less popular, at least in this society, because many young people are becoming more self-centred. They seem to think less about families and more about their own needs. Perhaps in the future this will make them less willing to make a major commitment like marriage, less willing to take responsibility.

IELTS Speaking Section

4. Reduce simple grammar mistakes

Constant, simple grammar mistakes may not affect communication but create an impression that your language level is lower than it probably is. You need to sound as much like a native speaker as possible. This example shows the differences clearly:

With grammar mistakes	Without grammar mistakes
Q: Which other language would you like to learn? **A:** *I like learn French* **Q:** Why? **A:** *It **is interested** language. My **father speak** French. He **learn** it when **he's** a child I like to **talk him** in French.*	**Q:** Which other language would you like to learn? **A:** *I'd really like to learn French* **Q:** Why? **A:** *It is such an interesting language. Actually, my father speaks French. He learnt it when he was a child. I'd really like to be able to talk with him in French.*

5. Use a good variety of vocabulary

Try to avoid repeating the same simple words, as the assessor will realise you lack word choice, and can't express meaning with precision. Using a variety of vocabulary creates interest and precision. Example - <u>Speaker 2</u> sounds more mature and engaging.

Speaker 1: My dog is nice. He's a very nice pet. He likes nice walks. It's nice to walk with him every day. Every day I go with him for a walk.

Speaker 2: My dog has a very friendly nature and is a very loving pet. He really enjoys his walk every day, and I get a great deal of pleasure from these daily outings as well.

6. Use up-to-date idioms or colloquial vocabulary <u>occasionally</u>

Idioms can add variety, too, used very occasionally, as these examples shows:

Q: Do you like studying in Australia
A: I still feel a bit **like a fish out of water**, even after more than a year here.

Q: Do you still play tennis?
A: No, I've had **to call it a day** temporarily, as I've got final exams soon.

Strategy IV - Pay attention to all aspects of pronunciation

Pronunciation is vital but complex. The better your pronunciation, the more easily you are understood and you connect better with the assessor. If your pronunciation is weak, try these adjustments.

1. Use chunking

'Chunking' involves speaking in blocks of words and then taking a tiny pause. It helps to build a slightly slower rhythm consisting of clear blocks of meaning, and helps the listener.

2. Practise good stress and rhythm

Sentence stress

Remember to stress the main information-carrying parts of your responses. The classes of words that are usually stressed are nouns, verbs, adverbs or adjectives. Other classes that aren't stressed are prepositions, articles, linking expressions, pronouns. They are usually spoken quickly and softly, leading up to the parts of sentences that are stressed.

Word stress

Be careful to pinpoint correct stress inside words (e.g. souven**IR,** not sou**VE**nir; **MAN**ager not man**AG**er; **IN**ternet, not in**TER**net).

3. Inject 'life' with good intonation to create 'voice music'

To introduce more intonation ('voice music') into your responses, use a rising intonation when you ask a question or show your surprise or excitement. Use a falling intonation at the end of statement sentences.

 *Scan the QR code to access some great **extra help with Pronunciation** in the Treasure Chest or visit https://ielts-blog.com/treasure-chest*

Solving Problems with the Speaking Test

While preparing for the Speaking test some parts of the test may seem challenging. Don't worry, this is normal! By tackling issues early, you will reduce their impact in the real test. Here are some common problems.

Problem 1: I didn't understand one of the questions in Part 1.

Problem 2: My mind goes blank because I'm nervous.

Problem 3: I 'freeze' when speaking to this stranger (the assessor).

Problem 4: The thinking time I need before I speak in English causes short silences.

Problem 5: I don't want to talk about the Part 2 topic or don't know anything about it.

Problem 6: I didn't make notes before the short talk in Part 2.

Problem 7: I didn't talk for two minutes in Part 2.

Problem 8: I didn't understand one of the questions in Part 3.

Problem 9: My assessor seems uninterested or stops me before I have finished.

 Scan the QR code to download the **solutions for these problems** from the Treasure Chest or visit https://ielts-blog.com/treasure-chest

SPEAKING CHECKPOINT TEST

Get Ready for the Checkpoint Test

You should by now have a better idea of the ways you respond to an IELTS Speaking test interview and how to respond better in that situation. You will also be more aware of the types of question or topic you may need to respond to in your actual IELTS test, as well as having some helpful strategies to boost your score.

Feeling confident?

If you feel confident, move straight on to the IELTS Speaking Checkpoint test on the next page. Before you start, think about your profile as a speaker of English - your strengths and weaknesses when taking this part of the IELTS test.

 *Scan the QR code to access the **Speaking Checkpoint Test recording** in the Treasure Chest or visit https://ielts-blog.com/treasure-chest*

Feeling less confident?

If you are still struggling to master many of the aspects of spoken English expected in the IELTS interview, your best strategy is to go back and repeat the Entry test again.

Doing the Entry test again has several advantages:

- You will be familiar with what the questions are going to be and can focus more easily on improving your actual responses
- You will be more relaxed and will feel more confident to form your responses with enriched variety of language use
- You will remember your previous responses and will have a better sense of how to improve them

After repeating the Entry test, try to score yourself again. Was your performance better? In all four areas that are assessed or only in some?

Move on to the Speaking Checkpoint test after a few days, or when you feel ready.

IELTS SPEAKING CHECKPOINT TEST

Test Instructions

1. Listen to the **Introduction** and **Part 1** and respond to each question. **Pause** the recording before answering each question.

2. After the introduction to Part 2, **pause** the recording for **one minute** to make notes.

3. After the one minute, **start** the recording again. After you hear, 'Could you start talking now, please', **pause** the recording again and start talking for a minimum of one and a maximum of two minutes.

4. **Start** the recording again after two minutes maximum, listen to and answer the rounding off question. Then just **continue** as the interview moves into **Part 3**.

5. **Pause** the recording before answering each question in Part 3.

Test Questions

PART 1

Let's talk about where you live.

- What kind of apartment or house are you living in at the moment?
- And what do you like about your house?
- How far is your house from public transport and shops?
- If you could change one thing in your house, what would it be?

Let's go on to talk about eating now.

- What foods do you eat that are really healthy?
- Do you eat sweet things very often? Why?
- Are you eating healthier food now than you were when you were a child?

I'd like you to talk about your evenings now.

- How do you usually spend your evenings?
- Are you ever tired in the evening?
- Do you sometimes eat late in the evening?

PART 2

> Talk about an occasion when someone gave you some money. You should say
>
> - who gave the money to you
> - why they gave it to you
> - what you used the money for
>
> and say why the money was important to you.

Rounding-off question: Do people often give you money?

PART 3

You've been talking about some money that someone gave you and I'd like to discuss with you a few more questions related to this topic.

Let's consider money as a gift.

- When do people often give money to others in your culture?
- Do you think giving a present is better than giving money?
- Well, do you think parents give money to children more often now than in the past?

Let's talk now about money and personal values.

- Why do you think so many people these days want to be rich?
- What about you, could you live a simple life in the future and live without money?

Let's talk a little about money in the world.

- What is your explanation for why the wealth gap between rich and poor people is becoming wider in many societies?

That is the end of the Checkpoint Speaking test.

Finished the Checkpoint test?

Now you have finished the Checkpoint Test, listen to the responses of another test taker to the same interview, and compare them with your own.

 *Scan the QR code to access the **recording of Pragnesh's Speaking Test** in the Treasure Chest or visit https://ielts-blog.com/treasure-chest*

The approximate scores Pragnesh would get in IELTS are listed in the table below. Using them a guide, give yourself a score for your own responses in the table below.

Assessment Criteria	What it means	Your score (0-9)	Pragnesh's score (0-9)
Fluency and Coherence (FC)	A high score means the test taker can keep speaking without much hesitation, pausing between words or self-correction. Their answers should be appropriate and well-developed and their ideas organised and connected using a range of linking words.		7
Lexical Resource (LR)	A high score means the test taker can convey their thoughts clearly using a good variety of appropriate words and expressions, as well as paraphrasing particular words or phrases they can't remember while talking.		6
Grammatical Range and Accuracy (GRA)	A high score means the test taker's sentences are mostly grammatically correct and they are able to use complex as well as simple sentences.		6
Pronunciation (Pron)	A high score means the listener can understand the test taker easily. This includes correct pronunciation, intonation (raising and lowering the voice appropriately) and the use of chunking - organising your sentences into small, manageable spoken units and pauses between them.		7
Total Score	(FC + LR + GRA + Pron) / 4		6.5

Once you have decided your own scores on all four criteria for your interview, check the Treasure Chest for our detailed "Analysis and Scores for Pragnesh" to understand how IELTS Speaking is marked and what affects the score in each assessment criterion. Then read "How could Pragnesh have done better?" to understand what can be done to improve each score.

Repeat the review process to build further awareness of your ongoing weaknesses, and to chart how your test techniques and speaking skills have improved. Repeat the checkpoint test a few days later.

Your Final Challenge - our Complete IELTS Exit Test

Now you have completed the entry tests and checkpoint tests for all four parts of IELTS and have practised all the question and task types, your final challenge is to take our Exit test.

You should take all four parts of the IELTS Exit test at the same sitting (Listening, Reading, Writing and Speaking), and then score your performance on all parts.

You will recognise the Listening and Reading sections of the Exit test, and this will help you, but the questions will be different.

Repeating a test is not wasting your time

Again, we recommend repeating the Exit test after a few days. Redoing a test is not a waste of time but an opportunity to monitor and improve your strategies and performance while feeling more relaxed.

Thank You

Thank you for using IELTS Test Mastery. If you have worked through our book systematically, you will surely be closer to that all-important score. We wish you all the best for your IELTS test!

Stephen and Simone

COMPLETE
IELTS EXIT TEST

How to take the Exit test

Your IELTS journey

Your journey through this book has now reached its **final challenge - a full IELTS test.** Your goal is to take all the elements - Listening, Reading, Writing and Speaking together, just as you would in the actual IELTS. If you know that your local IELTS test centre conducts the Speaking part on a different day, you should carry out this exit test exactly as it is offered locally.

This is your chance to show your **IELTS Test Mastery**. Naturally, you still won't have complete mastery of the IELTS Test, but **having worked through** the sections in **this book** you should feel greater awareness and control of the IELTS test situation, and of the kinds of questions and tasks you will need to deal with. **Greater mastery leads to greater confidence, calmness and control**.

How to proceed

1. Start with the Exit Listening test. To build your confidence, we have used the same recordings as we used for the Checkpoint Test, so you will remember the situations and some of the language, but the questions are entirely different. After finishing, don't score your performance yet.

Take a short break, just a few minutes

2. Move on immediately to the Exit Reading test. Again, we have used the same passages as in the Checkpoint Test but with totally different questions. This will help to keep you calmer and more relaxed. **Keep strictly to the time allowed (60 minutes)**. Again, don't score your performance yet.

Take another short break

3. Next, do the Exit Writing Test. This is a completely new test but you should be reasonably confident after the Listening and Reading sections. **Keep strictly to the time limit of 60 minutes** (20 minutes for Task 1 and 40 minutes for Task 2).

Take a final break

4. Finally, do the Exit Speaking test. Remember to **use the pause button** between questions on the recording and to **keep to the timing** of the Speaking test during Part 2 (1 minute preparation, and 1-2 minutes for your talk) and Part 3 (about 3-4 minutes in total). **Record your Speaking test if you possibly can** for later review.

 *Scan the QR code to access the **Listening Exit Test recording and a blank answer sheet** in the Treasure Chest or visit https://ielts-blog.com/treasure-chest*

START the Exit Test

When you are ready and comfortable, **START** the Listening test on the next page and then move through the other test parts.

After completing the whole test, read page 226 for guidance on scoring. Remember, **don't score your performance until you have completely finished the Exit Test.**

LISTENING TEST

Test Instructions

 Listen to the recording straight through, **ONCE** only (total audio time: 30 min). Answer the questions while listening to each section. At the end of the test, you will have another ten minutes to transfer your answers to the Answer sheet.

PART 1   *Questions 1 – 10*

Questions 1 – 5

Complete the Seafront Backpacker hostel enquiry form.

Write **NO MORE THAN 2 WORDS AND/OR A NUMBER** for each answer.

Seafront Backpacker Hostel
Bay View Heights

Guest Form

Guest's Current Address: **Seaview Hotel   EXAMPLE**   15 Esplanade, Dune Beach

Family Name of guest (**1**) _____   First Name (**2**) _____

Phone No. (**3**) _____   No of nights required (**4**) _____

Cost per night: Dormitory **A**: $18 **B**: $15   Weekly Cost (7 nights) (**5**) $ _____

Questions 6 – 10

Choose the correct letter **A**, **B** or **C**.

6 Each bathroom at the hostel has...

    A no shower but hot water all the time
    B a shower and hot water all the time
    C a shower, and hot water sometimes

7 Which facilities are free?

    A Breakfast and internet
    B Breakfast and car parking
    C Towels and bike parking

8 He recommends the road from Dune Beach to Selby because...

    A it's near the hotel
    B it's not busy
    C it's safer for cycling

9 The hostel is located:

    A up a hill on the sea front
    B in a retirement home on the beach
    C along a right turn off Beach Road

10 Which animal is known to be a problem to the caller?

    A fox
    B dog
    C cat

PART 2   Questions 11 – 20

Complete the notes below.

Use **ONE WORD AND/OR A NUMBER** for each answer.

Name of machine	Positive (+) features	Negative (–) features	Overall Assessment
Coffee Supreme	can brew 4+ cups of mild/strong coffee water filtration system (**11**) _____ the taste overflow protection/ drip stop parts easy to (**12**) _____	no auto grinder (**13**) _____ watt electrical system	good value for money but (**14**) _____ performance
Café Delight	combines a (**15**) _____ coffee maker with an espresso machine steam nozzle + frothing attachment	machine is (**16**) _____ and large	flexible and (**17**) _____
Coffeetime Automatic	can make different (**18**) _____ has electronic disc to calculate water needs automatically auto clean/descale	(**19**) _____ and too large	bulky but uses current (**20**) _____ well

PART 3 **Questions 21 – 30**

Question 21

Choose **TWO** correct letters from **A, B, C** or **D**.

21 Which TWO are purposes of the Student Support Service?

    A to improve students' independence
    B to carry out some of the study for the students
    C to encourage students to make judgments
    D to help students to build relationships

Questions 22 – 26

Answers the questions below about Wilson's study problems.

Write **NO MORE THAN ONE WORD AND/OR A NUMBER** for each answer.

What is Wilson's main problem?	22 _____
What part of an assignment is often not clear to him?	23 _____
With which aspect of his essay problems will the special session help?	24 _____
What is <u>one</u> of Wilson's other problems with essay writing?	25 _____
With whom can Wilson talk about the drafts of his essays?	26 _____

Questions 27 – 30

Complete the Report on Grace's problems.

Write **NO MORE THAN ONE WORD AND/OR A NUMBER** for each answer.

REPORT

Grace has difficulty keeping up with (**27**) _____ on her Nursing Course.

She says that lecturers speak too quickly and are not always (**28**) _____.

She thinks that the recording of lectures (**29**) _____ time.

Grace is not sleeping well; seems worried about her family.
I suggested that she should talk to a counsellor from a different cultural (**30**) _____.

I offered to help her to make the appointment.

PART 4 Questions 31 – 40

Choose the correct letter **A, B** or **C** according to what the lecturer says:

31 Management research now understands that...

- A organisations need a structure
- B feelings affect relationships significantly
- C workplace relationships can only be effective with rules

32 Emotional intelligence is...

- A an aspect of IQ
- B a range of abilities linked to feelings
- C an important management task

33 Empathy essentially involves...

- A imagining another's feelings
- B understanding certain conditions
- C feeling natural enough

34 Managing other people's feelings is helpful to...

- A self-motivation
- B popularity of the organisation
- C leadership skills

35 In a happy workplace, people are...

- A intelligent and technically competent
- B cooperative and respectful
- C aware of the importance of quality

Questions 36 – 40

Complete the sentences below. Write **ONE WORD ONLY** from the lecture for each answer.

A manager with a healthy self-image will probably be a (**36**) _____ influence in workplaces.

Our perceived self is our inner (**37**) _____ of ourselves.

Our desired self focuses on what is (**38**) _____ within ourselves.

Our presented selves require us to behave according to what is (**39**) _____ by others.

The three aspects of the self are not performed individually, but (**40**) _____.

READING TEST

Test Instructions

You have **ONE HOUR** to answer 40 questions in three sections. You must transfer your answers to the Answer sheet during this time. Allow approximately 20 minutes for each section.

READING PASSAGE 1

Read Passage 1 below and answer **questions 1 – 13**

Why are women becoming unhappier?

A The 21st century American woman enjoys the benefit of more, and better domestic appliances, higher incomes, more control over fertility and relationships, and better education. So it is paradoxical that the improvements in the objective situation of women in the USA and other industrialised countries over the past 40 years have not been accompanied by perceptions of increased happiness. In fact, women seem to perceive themselves to be both less happy than they were in the 70s and less happy now than men.

B Stephenson and Wolfer's review of the sociological data indicates that, historically, women reported higher levels of subjective well-being than men. By the twenty-first century, women reported happiness levels on a par with, or perhaps lower than those reported by men. Compounding this trend among adults, the US Monitoring the Future study, which since 1976 has been surveying approximately 15,000 US twelfth graders each year about their attitudes, has found that young men have raised levels of happiness, while young women have become slightly less happy.

C Sociologists seem to be unsure about the reasons. Data are inconclusive in terms of whether women now work more hours than men as a result of social changes. However, Hochschild and Machung's work hints at the possibility that women still carry the emotional responsibility in the home and that this is now more challenging for them. Increased divorce rates and growing numbers of children born out of wedlock may have added to women's emotional burdens. Yet, research data tend to suggest that levels of happiness are not significantly different between those women with, and those without children. Other sociologists like Kimball and Willis suggest that the hopefulness and idealism that accompanied the growth of the women's movement in the 70's have gradually weakened. Perhaps connected to this, the largest decline in happiness among women was among the group that had attended university, though this reflects the

steadily increasing proportion of women who have been attending college across the past 40 years. In fact, irrespective of the age, marital, labour market, or fertility status of the group analysed, data suggest that both the absolute decline in happiness among women in the United States, and the even larger decline relative to men, seems to be widespread. In Europe, trends are similar with perhaps an even greater decline in the happiness of women relative to men. The attempt to find a critical, explanatory variable has so far proven elusive, however.

D   With which aspects of their lives are women now less satisfied? A number of survey questions have explored satisfaction across a number of domains: work, financial situation, family, health, and job satisfaction. Women remain similarly satisfied with their work when compared with both the past, and with men. With financial situation perceptions have changed. Women begin the sampling period reporting financial satisfaction that is similar to that for men. However, women's financial satisfaction declines through the 80s and 90s, and, by the end of the sample period, women are substantially less satisfied with their household financial situation than are men. What is more, the magnitude of the decline in women's satisfaction with their financial situation is similar to the decline in women's happiness overall.

E   On average, women are less happy with their marriage than men, and women have become less happy with their marriage over time. However, men have also become less happy with their marriage; thus, the gender gap in marital happiness has been largely stable. Marital happiness is more closely linked to general happiness for women, with the correlation between overall happiness and marital happiness being 0.4 for married men and 0.5 for married women. When asked to rate their health on a four-point scale from poor to excellent, women throughout the period report lower health satisfaction than do men. In contrast, men's subjective health assessment has not changed much over this period.

F   Returning to the teenagers, it seems that the subjective well-being of girls is falling and the well-being of boys rising. There appears to be increasing ambition among young women beyond the domestic sphere, with greater importance attached to being successful and being able to find steady work, or making a contribution to society. These data arguably suggest that women's life satisfaction may have become more complicated as women have increased the number of domains in which they wish to succeed. Moreover, the data point to rising pressures beyond the much-discussed work-family trade-off.

G   One possibility is that broad social shifts such as those brought on by the changing role of women in society fundamentally alter what measures of subjective well-being are actually capturing, leading to falling average satisfaction as it becomes difficult to achieve the same degree of satisfaction in multiple domains. Perhaps the puzzle is less one of finding out why women see themselves as less happy and more one of unravelling why men's happiness has not declined in line with women's happiness.

Questions 1 – 5

Reading Passage 1 has 7 paragraphs, **A – G**.

Which paragraph contains the following information?

Write the correct letter, **A – G**, in boxes **1 – 5** on your answer sheet.

1   The proposition that women may be less happy because they no longer have the same feminist, political dreams of 40 years ago.

2   The view that for women to be as satisfied with their lives is more complex because of the larger number of fields in which they want to excel.

3   The parallel size of the reduction in women's satisfaction with their financial circumstances and their general happiness.

4   The view that perhaps it may be more important to focus research on the explanation of why men's happiness levels have held up better.

5   The seeming contradiction between the improvement in women's actual living conditions and the decline in how happy they perceive themselves to be.

Questions 6 –10

Do the following statements agree with the information given in Reading Passage 1?

In boxes 6 –10 on your answer sheet write

> **TRUE**   if the statement agrees with the information
> **FALSE**   if the statement contradicts the information
> **NOT GIVEN**   if there is no information on this

6   Younger women are feeling a sense of declining happiness.

7   It makes little difference to perceptions of happiness if a woman is a mother or not.

8   Twelfth-grader young men view themselves as healthier than their young, female counterparts.

9   The link between marital happiness and overall happiness is stronger for men than for women.

10   Men's perceptions of their health have been more stable than women's across the survey period.

Questions 11-13

Complete the summary below.

Choose **ONE WORD ONLY** from the passage for each answer.

Write your answers in boxes 11-13 on your answer sheet.

Women in the USA (**11**) _____ themselves to be less happy than 40 years ago, despite improvements in their lives. Men's levels of happiness have not (**12**) _____ to the same extent. The explanation for this is still a (**13**) _____.

READING PASSAGE 2

Read Passage 2 below and answer **Questions 14 – 26**

The changing vocal world of the humpback whale

A   In the dark world of the world's oceans, whales depend on echolocation – the use of sound for navigation. Only 1 per cent of surface light travels to a depth of 100 meters; at 600 meters the sun's illumination equals that of starlight. Lacking an external ear, they detect sound waves via a fat pad between mandible and middle ear. Among the cetaceans, humpback whales are recognized by scientists as one of the most vocally diverse and exciting species. The cetologist, Peter Beamish, tested the navigational skills of humpback whales in the dark. After building a maze in a Newfoundland bay for a humpback rescued from a fishing net, he blindfolded the whale with rubber drain plungers. Before being set free, the humpback managed to find its way through the maze, thereby demonstrating the effectiveness of echolocation.

B   In 1967, the biologist Roger Payne started making and analysing recordings of the sounds of humpbacks off Bermuda. Working from hundreds of hours of tape recordings taken on the breeding ground, Payne contended that the sounds they heard were more than idle chatter. They described the sounds as notes uttered in succession which together formed a recognizable sequence or pattern in time. In other words, they were songs with distinctive themes. All the whales in a breeding group appeared to sing the same songs, over and over again.

C   Scientists have been studying humpback whale songs for nearly fifty years, but there are strange things about them which resist explanation. For instance, only the male whales sing these amazing songs, so it is generally assumed that the song is to attract the attention of females. However, no one has ever seen a female whale approach a singing male. Instead, other males seem to be more interested. When they approach the singer, he stops singing, and the two males go off silently together for a little while, and then they separate.

D   In any year, whales sing identical songs in Hawaii and Mexico, breeding areas that are 4,500 kilometres apart. How is this possible? Perhaps they hear the songs across long distances or learn them during the summer months, when different groups gather in the north to feed. More remarkable than the geographic consistency is the change in calls over time. Slight variations in the songs occur each year. But, as with evolution, these changes can make huge leaps in a short time. Variation in whale songs is evidence that cetaceans have culture, which can change over time and vary across oceans. The Australian biologist, Mike Noad, and colleagues, found evidence of a 'cultural revolution' in the Southern Hemisphere. In 1996 two male humpbacks from the Indian Ocean arrived in the Pacific with a new song. Within two years, all the Pacific males had changed their tune, picking up the migrants' songs. An explanation of this switch is not so straightforward. A preference for novelty is one possibility, though this theory seems to be contradicted by the observation that all whales in a particular area sing the same song in a given year. Although the cause of this dramatic change is still unclear, the knowledge that cetacean cultures endure and change over time, and that culture is not the unique domain of humans is likely to radically transform perception of these mammals.

E Unfortunately, whales, and an understanding of their calls, are under a new threat. Noise that degrades information exchange comes in many forms, and it may change the use of a communication system and possibly derail communication all together. Dependency on sound makes whales vulnerable to the rising level of noise in the oceans. The number of cargo ships has tripled in the past 75 years, with larger vessels plying the seas each year. These human-generated, chronic sounds are akin to a smog of acoustic noise. Fishermen employing depth finders and acoustical gear in their search for fish add to this noise. The constant underwater din, which can impact whales' ability to hunt and reproduce, is punctuated by intense pulses from seismic air guns, used to plot oil and gas deposits along the ocean shelf. Among the loudest sounds produced by humans, these pulses reach across entire oceans and may be responsible for recent whale strandings.

F Naval exercises using high-decibel mid-frequency sonar for antisubmarine training can also harm whales. Mass strandings of beaked whales have occurred around the world after military tests. In 2000, 13 beaked whales and two minkes stranded in the Bahamas after the US Navy deployed mid-frequency sonar. Four of the whales had unusual haemorrhages near their ears. In 2002, 14 beaked whales were stranded in the Canary Islands after a test. Ten of them had gas bubbles in their blood vessels, clear evidence of decompression sickness. The whales may have reacted to the ear-splitting noises by heading for the surface too quickly, disoriented by the sonar. Given that symptoms of the bends have never been found in these deep-diving whales, it is also possible that the noises caused the bubbles to form in the bloodstream of vulnerable whales. There is evidence that, in the laboratory, cetaceans attempt to avoid noise and increase breathing rates, a sign of stress. In the acoustic smog of the modern ocean, there may be nowhere for dolphins and whales to go. Noise can also affect communication. Humpback whales change their songs in the presence of active sonar, extending their calls to compensate for the acoustic interference on their breeding grounds. The situation is unlikely to improve in the near future.

Complete IELTS Exit Test

Questions 14 – 17

Reading Passage 2 has 6 paragraphs, A – F.

Choose the correct headings for paragraphs **A – D** from the list below.

Write the correct number, **i-viii**, in boxes 14-17 on your answer sheet.

List of Headings

i	The darkness of the ocean's waters
ii	Song variation as evidence of whale society
iii	Some mysterious features of whale song
iv	Understanding whale song
v	humpback whales detect sound
vi	Sounds and distance
vii	Males and females
viii	Recording of whale song
ix	The threat of noise

EXAMPLE	ANSWER
Paragraph E	___ ix ___

14   Paragraph A   _____
15   Paragraph B   _____
16   Paragraph C   _____
17   Paragraph D   _____

Questions 18 – 21

*Choose the correct letter, **A**, **B**, **C** or **D**.*

18 How did Roger Payne characterise the sounds in his early recordings?

    A   They were signs that whales were chattering when they were feeling lazy.

    B   The sounds were only made when whales were breeding.

    C   The sounds seemed to reflect repeated topics of musical 'conversation'.

    D   The sounds were successful in helping whales to recognise one another.

19 What does the writer say about humpback whale song in terms of male and female reactions?

    A   Songs are definitely mating calls initiated by males.

    B   Males are interested in following females when the song is being used.

    C   When they hear a male singing, other males want to sing.

    D   The songs seem to lead to a strange silent pattern of behaviour among male.

20 What does the writer say about the quality of noise in today's oceans?

    A   Noise from ships is creating a clear grading of sounds under the ocean.

    B   The noise is a confusing blend of sounds which is ceaseless.

    C   Noise in the ocean today is similar to that made by trains on railways.

    D   Sounds of fish add further volume to the ocean noise.

21 Which is the most likely combination of explanations for whale strandings, according to the writer?

    A   Stress and military testing

    B   Sonar pulses and decompression sickness

    C   Ears splitting and avoidance behaviour

    D   Faster breathing rates and haemorrhages

Questions 22 – 26

Complete the summary of paragraphs **D**, **E** and **F** (questions 22-26 below).

Use **ONE** word from the list (**A – O** below) for each answer.

Write the correct letter, **A – O**, in the boxes 22-26 on your answer sheet.

Whales sing identical songs across long distances. But, slight changes in the songs occur each year. Such **(22)** _____ of whale songs is evidence that cetaceans have culture, which can vary across oceans. The knowledge that whale **(23)** _____ both endure and change indicates that culture is not just **(24)** _____ to humans. This is likely to transform how these mammals are perceived.

Increasing ocean noise seems to **(25)** _____ information exchange among whales and may disrupt communication altogether. The constant underwater din affects their hunting and breeding ability, and may be responsible for strandings.

Strandings have also occurred after military tests. The whales may have reacted to noise by **(26)** _____ too quickly. The situation is not likely to improve soon.

A	moderation	**B**	floating	**C**	lessen
D	species	**E**	numbers	**F**	effect
G	restricted	**H**	available	**I**	modification
J	damaged	**K**	societies	**L**	share
M	surfacing	**N**	groups	**O**	diving

READING PASSAGE 3

Read Passage 3 below and answer **Questions 27 – 40**.

Wave energy – a UK perspective

Waves are generated by the wind as it blows across the ocean surface. They travel great distances and so act as an efficient energy transport mechanism across thousands of kilometres. The energy can be captured by various devices, which produce enough movement either of air or water to drive generators that convert the energy into electricity.

A The energy contained in ocean waves can potentially provide an unlimited source of renewable energy. Ocean waves are created by the interaction of wind with the surface of the sea and the UK has wave power levels that are amongst the highest in the world. The initial solar power level of about 100W/m2 is concentrated to an average wave power level of 70kW/metre of crest length. This figure rises to an average of 170kW/metre of crest length during the winter, and to more than 1,000kW/metre during storms. Wave energy converters extract and convert this energy into a useful form. The conversion usually makes use of either mechanical motion or fluid pressure, and there are numerous techniques for achieving it. The mechanical energy is then converted to electrical power using a generator. Wave energy converters can be deployed either on the shoreline or in the deeper waters offshore. East-facing sites in the UK are unsuitable because of the limited energy associated with easterly winds, while bottom friction reduces power levels where the water depth is less than 80 metres. As a result, the inshore resource is usually only one-quarter or less of the deep-water resource.

B The three main types of wave power machines either sit on the shoreline or are free-floating.

Oscillating water column
An oscillating water column is a partially submerged, hollow structure that is installed in the ocean. It is open to the sea below the water line, enclosing a column of air on top of a column of water. Waves cause the water column to rise and fall, which in turn compresses and depresses the air column. This trapped air is allowed to flow to and from the atmosphere via a Wells turbine, which has the ability to rotate in the same direction regardless of the direction of the airflow. The rotation of the turbine generates electricity.

Buoyant moored device

A buoyant moored device floats on or just below the surface of the water and is moored to the sea floor. A wave power machine needs to resist the motion of the waves in order to generate power: part of the machine needs to move while another part remains still. In this type of device, the mooring is static and arranged such that the waves' motion will move only one part of the machine.

Hinged contour device

A hinged contour device is able to operate at greater depths than the buoyant moored device. Here, the resistance to the waves is created by the alternate motion of the waves, which raises and lowers different sections of the machine relative to each other, pushing hydraulic fluid through hydraulic pumps to generate electricity.

The main problem with wave power is that the sea is an unforgiving environment. An economically-viable wave power machine will need to generate power over a wide range of wave sizes, as well as withstand the largest and most severe storms and other potential problems such as algae, barnacles and corrosion.

C   Due to lack of long-term commercial operating experience, actual cost data is virtually non-existent. The estimates always show projected cost per kWh, falling over time due to better designs and increasing unit size. Given the state of technology there is little doubt that many designs can generate electricity but the key question is can they do so cheaply. It would be straightforward to build very strong devices capable of withstanding all the storm conditions expected - the difficulty is constructing at minimum capital cost and having minimum operating cost (for maintenance and repair) so that the overall cost of generation is kept as low as possible and is competitive with alternative forms of generation.

D   There are two wave power devices in the UK. Total installed capacity currently stands at 1.25 megawatts. The first type of device is the LIMPET (Land Installed Marine Powered Energy Transformer), a 500-kilowatt shoreline oscillating water column on the Scottish island of Islay. The second, the 750-kilowatt Pelamis sea snake, is an example of a hinged contour device. It is the first deep-water grid-connected trial and is currently installed at the European Marine Energy Centre in Scotland, where it has been undergoing testing.

E   Marine energy could provide around 20 per cent of the UK's electricity needs but only if there is sufficient investment in the appropriate technology. In the short-term the initial set-up costs of marine energy are high as it requires extensive research and development. Yet it is clear that sufficient investment now could lead to a strong UK marine energy sector. The UK is in prime position to accelerate commercial progress in the marine energy sector and secure economic value by selling marine energy devices, developing wave and tidal stream farms and creating new revenues from electricity generation.

F   Wind-generated waves on the ocean surface have a total estimated power of 90 million gigawatts worldwide. Due to the direction of the prevailing winds and the size of the Atlantic Ocean, the UK has wave power levels that are among the highest in the world. Wave energy has the potential to provide as much renewable energy as the wind industry.

Questions 27 – 30

The reading passage has 6 paragraphs **A – F**.

Which paragraph, **A – F**, contains the following information?

Write the correct letter, **A – F**, in boxes 27-30 on your answer sheet.

27 Some discussion of the economic potential of wave energy in the UK.

28 General data on rates of power relative to wave height and length.

29 A brief analysis of factors affecting economic viability.

30 Current operational power capacity.

Questions 31 – 35

Do the following statements agree with the information given in Reading Passage 3?

In boxes **31 – 35** on your answer sheet write

> **YES**   if the statement agrees with the claims of the writer
> **NO**   if the statement contradicts the claims of the writer
> **NOT GIVEN**   if it is impossible to say what the writer thinks about this

31 The sea bed and restricted water depth both have an impact on the energy potential of waves.

32 Generators are more effective with the buoyant-moored device.

33 Wave energy devices need to be able to cope with plants or organisms which might attach themselves to the machinery.

34 Projections usually assume unit costs will increase as innovative, larger machines are developed.

35 One of the devices currently being tested is joined to the main electricity network.

Questions 36 – 40

To which device does each statement apply?

Choose one device from the box below and write the correct letter, **A – C**, next to questions **36 – 40**.

A	Oscillating water column
B	Buoyant moored device
C	Hinged contour device

36 This device is attached to the sea bed and is usually visible above the water level.

37 This device enables independent movement and varies the height of its different parts.

38 This device is tube-like and some of it is not visible above the level of the sea.

39 This device produces energy largely from alternation of air pressure.

40 This device relies principally on the variation in wave movement to produce fluid pressure which is then converted into energy

WRITING TEST

TASK 1

You should spend about 20 minutes on this task.

The following table shows average daily water use in households in the USA before and after the application of water efficiency measures.

Summarise the information by selecting and reporting the key features, and make any relevant comparisons.

Average daily water consumption USA (in gallons)

Year / Use	2011	2012 (After water efficiency measures)
Shower	11.6	8.8
Washing machine	15.0	10.0
Dishwasher	1.0	0.7
Toilet	18.5	8.2
Bath	1.2	1.2
Water leaks	9.5	4.0
Household taps	10.9	10.8
Other uses	1.6	1.6
TOTAL	69.3	45.3

Write at least 150 words.

TASK 2

You should spend about 40 minutes on this task.

Write about the following topic:

> **Some people believe that spending money and living for today makes more sense than saving for the future.**
>
> **Do you agree?**
>
> **Give reasons for your answer and include any relevant ideas from your own knowledge or experience.**

Write at least 250 words.

SPEAKING TEST

Test Instructions

 Scan the QR code to access the **Speaking Exit Test recording** in the Treasure Chest or visit https://ielts-blog.com/treasure-chest

PLEASE record your own interview, if possible, for better self-assessment

1. Listen to the **Introduction** and **Part 1** and respond to each question. **Pause** the recording before answering each question.

2. After the introduction to Part 2, **pause** the recording for **one minute** to make notes.

3. After the one minute, **start** the recording again. After you hear, 'Could you start talking now, please', **pause** the recording again and start talking for a minimum of one and a maximum of two minutes.

4. **Start** the recording again after two minutes maximum, listen to and answer the rounding off question. Then just **continue** as the interview moves into **Part 3**.

5. **Pause** the recording before answering each question in **Part 3**.

Test Questions

PART 1

Let's talk about where you live.
- In what kind of house or apartment are you living at the moment?
- Is the location a good one?
- In what ways is your neighbourhood improving or getting worse?
- What changes would most improve the area where you live?

Let's go on to talk about dogs now.
- Do you like dogs?
- What kind of dogs frighten you a little?
- Is a dog better than a cat as a pet, do you think?
- Why are some dogs really noisy and others quiet?

Let's move on to talk about mobile phones now.
- How many mobile phones have you owned?
- What is the most annoying thing about your mobile phone?
- Do you use most of the functions on your mobile phone, or only a few?
- Is the mobile phone dangerous to your health?

PART 2

> Talk about one of the best days of your life. You should say
>
> - when this day was
> - what you did on that day and with whom
> - how you felt about it then and how you feel about that day now
>
> And say why you have chosen to talk about this occasion rather than others

Rounding-off question: Do you have many really special memories from your life, or just a few?

PART 3

You've just been talking one of the best days in your life, and I'd like to discuss with you a few more questions related to the same topic.

Let's consider first of all special days.

- Tell me about one of the most special days celebrated in your country each year.

- Would you say that national celebrations in your country today are less important to young people than perhaps they were in the past?

Let's move on to discuss the best nations in the world.

- When you compare your country with others, which other nations seem better than yours and why?

- So, do you think life in your country is going to get even better in the future?

Let's move on finally to consider making the world a better place.

- To what extent do you think a world organisation, like the United Nations, could actually create a better world if it had more power?

- So, do you think the world will be a better place in the future, or are the best days of our planet already in the past?

That is the end of the Exit test.

Score, Review then Practise

Score

Score all test parts <u>after</u> completion of the whole test, as in the actual IELTS.

For the Listening and Reading Exit tests, check the answers in the IELTS Answers section at the end of this book.

For the Writing and Speaking parts, use the assessment criteria on pages 99-100 and 169, or ask an IELTS teacher or tutor to help you.

Review

Review your performance on all four parts, just as you did with the Entry and Checkpoint tests and compare your Exit test scores to those in the Entry and Checkpoint tests.

This is an opportunity to judge how your performance was affected by doing the full test. These questions might help:

- Did you find that tiredness affected your performance or concentration in the Writing test?
- Do you now think that you need to change any of your test strategies?
- Were you able to complete both Writing test tasks properly in the time allowed?
- Was your language use too repetitive during the Speaking test and your responses too short?

Practise

We truly believe that **doing a test a second time is really beneficial**, so after a few days, try the Exit test again to gain further insights into your strengths, weaknesses and strategies.

Good luck with your actual IELTS test! You can do it!

ANSWERS

WHAT'S INSIDE:

- Listening Answers
- Reading Answers
- Writing Answers
- Speaking Answers

Answers

Listening Tests Answers

Question.	Entry Test Answers	Checkpoint Test Answers	Exit Test Answers
1	3	15	Wong
2	brakes	014830579	Jacqui
3	study	12	014830579
4	1500	15	7
5	88	father	90
6	red	C	B
7	bike	B	A
8	city	C	C
9	mechanic	B	A
10	borrow	A	C
11	B	mild	improves
12	C	protection	replace
13	A	automatic	750
14	C	value	limited
15	B	steam	regular
16	A	wide	bulky
17	C	flexible	convenient
18	B	electronic	drinks
19	B	kitchens	pricey / pricy
20	C	bulky	technology
21	A	B and D	A, D *(both needed)*
22	C	seminars	writing
23	E	ideas	title / titles
24	A	plan	planning
25	E	disorganised	structuring / structure / disorganised
26	B	draft	tutor
27	C	recording lectures	lectures / lecturer
28	B	embarrassed	clear
29	A	(not) sleeping / sleep	wastes
30	C	(a) counsellor / counsellors	background
31	top	feelings	B
32	typewriters	abilities	B
33	inefficiency	empathy	A
34	keyboard/layout	motivate	C
35	70	effective	B
36	50	C	positive
37	accuracy	A	view
38	speed	B	missing
39	20	C	expected
40	habit	B	interact / together

Listening Activities Answers

Activity 1		Activity 6	
1.	A	1.	533 East 67th St
2.	A	2.	93014269
3.	V	**Activity 7**	
4.	V	1.	Thursday(s)
5.	C	2.	8 / eight
6.	C	3.	ATSTIX
Activity 2		**Activity 8**	
1.	C	1.	B/bookshop
2.	B	2.	morning(s)
3.	A	3.	M/music
Activity 3		4.	B/beauty
1.	admission	5.	Thursday
2.	select	**Activity 9**	
3.	middle	1.	adopted
4.	design	2.	habit
5.	distributed	3.	efficiency
Activity 4		**Activity 10**	
1.	jams	1.	how long
2.	inefficiency (built-in)	2.	(brief) notes
3.	(the) left	3.	eye contact
4.	(It) improved / an improvement	4.	speaking slowly
Activity 5		**Activity 11**	
1.	372	9.	A
2.	11:30	10.	E
3.	bag	11.	C
4.	Singapore		

Note:
1. '/' means alternative answer
2. '( )' means optional part of the answer
3. Your answers must be spelled correctly. Misspelled answers get 0 marks.

Answers

Entry Reading Test Answers

Question No.	Answer	Question No.	Answer
1	free	21	N
2	compelled	22	Y
3	prohibited	23	Y
4	afflicted	24	NG
5	exhaustion	25	subjectively
6	swollen feet	26	benefits
7	fury	27	sensitive
8	her husband	28	F
9	rave culture	29	NG
10	D	30	T
11	C	31	F
12	A	32	T
13	E	33	T
14	B	34	primary
15	F	35	filtration
16	B	36	remote
17	C	37	buoyancy
18	B	38	stomachs
19	F	39	D
20	G	40	A

 Scan the QR code to access **Answer Help** in the Treasure Chest or visit https://ielts-blog.com/treasure-chest

Reading Activities Answers

Activity 1	
1.	vi
2.	iii
3.	viii
4.	vii
5.	i

Activity 2	
1.	A
2.	C
3.	D

Activity 3	
1.	electricity
2.	moved
3.	flood
4.	science
5.	consumer

Activity 4	
1.	C
2.	B
3.	D
4.	A

Activity 5	
1.	YES
2.	YES
3.	NOT GIVEN
4.	NO

Activity 6	
1.	C
2.	B
3.	E
4.	E
5.	D

Activity 7	
1.	$2.5 billion
2.	flooding/flooding in Gympie
3.	higher gates/floodgates/higher floodgates
4.	water crisis

Activity 8	
1.	I
2.	A
3.	P

Activity 9	
1.	FALSE
2.	TRUE
3.	TRUE
4.	NOT GIVEN
5.	TRUE
6.	TRUE
7.	TRUE
8.	FALSE

Activity 10	
1.	D
2.	G
3.	B
4.	H

Activity 11	
1.	devastated
2.	support
3.	solution
4.	150,000ML/water

Activity 12	
1.	damage/disintegration
2.	upstream
3.	weatherboard shed/shed
4.	bitter
5.	$200 million

Activity 13	
1.	stability
2.	evaporator
3.	particles
4.	pale tan
5.	vitamin D

Note:
1. The actual IELTS Reading test has only 40 questions numbered 1-40.
2. '/' means alternative answer.

Answers

Checkpoint Reading Test Answers

Question No.	Answer	Question No.	Answer
1	TRUE	21	C
2	FALSE	22	B
3	NOT GIVEN	23	D
4	FALSE	24	navigation
5	TRUE	25	blindfolded
6	happiness	26	sequence
7	unsure	27	resist
8	declined	28	NO
9	B	29	YES
10	E	30	NO
11	C	31	N
12	C	32	Y
13	G	33	B
14	A-iv	34	C
15	B-vi	35	A
16	C-i	36	C
17	D-iii	37	A
18	E-vii	38	C
19	F-viii	39	E
20	D	40	B

 Scan the QR code to access **Answer Help** *in the Treasure Chest or visit https://ielts-blog.com/treasure-chest*

Exit Reading Test Answers

Question No.	Answer	Question No.	Answer
1	C	21	A
2	F	22	I
3	D	23	D
4	G	24	G
5	A	25	C
6	TRUE	26	M
7	TRUE	27	E
8	NOT GIVEN	28	A
9	FALSE	29	C
10	TRUE	30	D
11	perceive	31	YES
12	declined / changed	32	NOT GIVEN
13	puzzle	33	YES
14	v	34	NO
15	viii	35	YES
16	iii	36	B
17	ii	37	C
18	C	38	A
19	D	39	A
20	B	40	C

Note:
1. '/' means alternative answer.

 *Scan the QR code to access **Answer Help** in the Treasure Chest or visit https://ielts-blog.com/treasure-chest*

Answers

Writing Practice Tests Answers

> **Entry Test**

Writing Task 1 Sample Response (Band 9)

The chart illustrates the quantities of tea and coffee that were imported by four different countries, Canada, the UK, the USA and Italy in 2015, measured in tonnes.

An overview of the data reveals two prominent trends. Firstly, the UK stands out as the largest importer of tea, whereas Canada imported the least amount of this beverage. Secondly, there was a noticeable preference for tea over coffee in almost all the countries except for Canada whose residents favoured coffee instead.

In more detail, the UK led with a substantial import of 12,000 tonnes of tea, which was higher than the USA's 8,000 tonnes. Italy imported 5,000 tonnes of tea, and Canada came last with 3,000 tonnes.

In contrast, when it comes to coffee imports, Canada reported the highest figure at 7,000 tonnes, closely followed by the USA with 6,000 tonnes. Meanwhile, Italy and the UK imported significantly lower amounts of coffee, at 4,000 and 3,000 tonnes respectively.

Writing Task 2 Sample Response (Band 9)

The concept of retirement has traditionally been associated with the notion of enjoying leisure time after years of work. However, in recent times, there has been a growing debate about whether people should continue working beyond the retirement age. In my opinion, individuals should continue working even after reaching retirement age due to the various advantages it brings.

Firstly, continuing work beyond retirement age promotes healthy aging. Engaging in meaningful work keeps individuals mentally stimulated and reduces the risk of age-related cognitive decline. Work also provides a sense of purpose and social interaction, which can combat loneliness and isolation often experienced by retirees. Research has shown that staying active and involved in the workforce can contribute to improved overall well-being and a higher quality of life in later years.

Secondly, working beyond the retirement age promotes the transfer of knowledge and skills between generations. Older workers possess valuable experience and expertise that can benefit younger generations. By remaining in the workforce, they can mentor and guide younger colleagues, fostering a culture of continuous learning and professional development. This intergenerational exchange of knowledge and skills contributes to the overall growth and productivity of organizations.

In conclusion, continuing work beyond retirement age offers numerous advantages both for individuals and society as a whole. It promotes healthy aging, provides and facilitates intergenerational collaboration. Encouraging and supporting individuals to remain in the workforce beyond retirement age can lead to a more inclusive, productive, and fulfilling society.

Checkpoint Test

Writing Task 1 Sample Response (Band 9)

The two plans show the changes that occurred to the layout of a museum between 2008 and 2012.

Overall, what can be clearly seen is that a large number of new facilities were added to the museum by 2012 and that its range of services has expanded.

In 2008, the museum had quite a bare layout with a simple entrance leading to a reception area. There was also a gallery and a shop on the ground floor. Adjacent to the reception there was a reading room and a cloak room right next to it. A staircase accessible from the reception is visible on the plan, implying that the museum has another level, however, the diagram only describes the ground floor.

A number of changes were made by 2012, including the addition of a terrace to the left of the original entrance. The ground floor saw the addition of a new restaurant right next to the terrace, and the reception area doubled as a cloak room. One of the significant changes was the addition of an elevator which replaced the original staircase. A café and a new exhibition room were added to the left of the reading room, and a children's play area was created where the cloak room used to be.

Writing Task 2 Sample Response (Band 9)

The shift from a past where the elderly were actively engaged in daily social and physical routines to a present where loneliness and health concerns are prevalent among the aged has become apparent nowadays. It raises many important questions about the causes of this alarming trend and the ways in which it can be tackled.

One key factor in the increasing isolation of seniors is the change in family structure and societal dynamics. As young people move to urban areas for job opportunities, older family members are often left in less populated areas, leading to reduced daily interaction with their loved ones and friends. Furthermore, the rise of individualism has lessened the emphasis on regular family gatherings. Personal goals have become a priority for many, and traditional practices like frequent family gatherings have taken a back seat. This means that older family members, who used to rely on such visits for social interaction, now often face long stretches of solitude. Another significant issue is the adoption of sedentary lifestyles. Unlike in the past when physical activity was common, modern conveniences have reduced the need for physical movement in almost every aspect of our lives.

To improve this situation, it is essential to encourage community engagement that involves the elderly in social activities and also provides opportunities for them to exercise, such as walking clubs or dance classes. Additionally, fostering intergenerational relationships can be beneficial. To illustrate, introducing programmes that connect the elderly with younger people can lead to meaningful exchanges and companionship, and the youth involved in these programmes could also help to teach the elderly digital skills to help them connect with friends and family online.

In conclusion, by addressing the root causes of social isolation and the health issues among the elderly, we can create a more supportive environment for our ageing population.

Answers

> **Exit Test**

Writing Task 1 Sample Response (Band 9)

The table shows the average domestic consumption of water in gallons in the USA between 2011 and 2012, before and after the introduction of water efficiency options.

It is evident that water efficiency measures in the USA made a major contribution to the saving of this precious resource, significantly reducing the overall water consumption.

In 2011 the use of the toilet and washing machine were the major drivers of water consumption each day, at 18.5 and 15 gallons respectively. Taking showers and using taps were next at 11.6 and 10.9 gallons, with water leaks surprisingly significant at 9.5 daily gallons. Baths and dishwashers were far less greedy in terms of daily use, at about 1 gallon.

By 2012 the situation had improved thanks to the implementation of greater water efficiency controls. Average daily water consumption from toilet use dropped by over 40% to 8.2 gallons, and for washing machines by a third to 10 gallons. Loss of water due to water leaks saw the highest pro rata improvement, falling by well over 50% to four gallons. Savings on showers, baths, dishwashers and other uses were much less significant.

Writing Task 2 Sample Response (Band 9)

The world is becoming increasingly unpredictable, making it difficult to sense what kind of future awaits us all. This is why, in my opinion, saving for the later years in life is imperative as reliance on state support seems ill-advised.

Living in the present, it must be said, has its attractions. The 'here and now' is the only reality that we can truly experience so it makes sense to enjoy it to the utmost. It is likely that savouring life fully in the present also helps to prevent depression and makes a person active and positive. Spending also helps to sustain the national economy.

On the other hand, to deny the global difficulties that may further define the future seems foolhardy. Already, climate change is altering lives at a deep level and with increasing speed. Mass migration, reduced area of land suitable to farm, artificial intelligence, ever-yawning gaps between the rich and the poor, lessening of social support from governments, all point to a future in which more challenging conditions will prevail.

Such conditions demand preparation now, and a significant part of that preparation is saving, putting money aside to protect yourself and your family. If you don't do this, who will? All workers with decent employment should ensure they are contributing towards a retirement pension, and finding other ways of guaranteeing their future wellbeing, through education, investment and simpler lifestyles. Extravagant consumption, though tempting, should be seen as outmoded.

To summarise, saving for the future makes complete sense given the global conditions in which we find ourselves. No one has a crystal ball, but to be unprepared for the future is to risk a sad and miserable old age, and the denial of living only in the present doesn't change this prospect.

Writing Activities Answers

Writing Task 1

Question Type 1 - Map	
Activity #	**Answer**
1	b
2	a
3	b
4	c
5	a
6	c
7	show, overall, modernised, were
8	task, summary, present, past
9	a, b, e
10	western, northern, eastern
11	c
12	b
13	by, along, with, in, for, to
14	modifications, introduced, separate, seating, patrons
15	c
16	See sample answer in the Treasure Chest

Question Type 2 - Process Diagram	
Activity #	**Answer**
1	a
2	shows / covers
3	1) the main <u>steps</u>, 2) in <u>buying</u> 3) <u>viewing</u> and making
4	steps / buying / issues
5	finding the right house, negotiating a price, making financial arrangements
6	The first step / After that / Once / As soon as / After / Once / Then / As soon as
7	<u>Present passive</u>: is rejected, is required, is made, is carried out / is paid / is cleared (Any two) <u>Present perfect passive</u>: has been chosen, has been accepted
8	1) Then affordable areas <u>are looked for</u>. 2) Next, a house <u>is chosen</u> and an offer <u>is made</u>. 3) If it is accepted, a 10% deposit <u>is paid</u>.
9	See sample answer in the Treasure Chest

Answers

Writing Task 1

Question Type 3 - Graph

Activity #	Answer
1	a
2	indicates
3	higher / less / than
4	a) ...across the period surveyed, b) ...across the years studied, c) ...across the months compared
5	increased / fell back / peaking / returned / recovering / steady
6	a
7	a, c
8	(1) marginally, (2) noticeably, (3) substantially, (4) massively
9	See sample answer in the Treasure Chest

Question Type 4 - Table

Activity #	Answer
1	The chart presents data on access to computers and the Internet, in Australia between 1998 and 2000 for two income levels - below, and above $50,000.
2	Overall, To summarise, It can be clearly seen that
3	Correct Answers: upper, much higher, lower, more rapidly
4	the corresponding percentages across the three years
5	incomes / falling / recovering / marginally / corresponding / double
6	1990 -> 1998; 87% ->37%; $5000 ->$50,000; 77, 69 and 71% -> 69,71 and 77%
7	Starting from', 'the figure increased slightly to', 'then', 'from', 'to', 'and then to'
8	1. the figures were much higher, 2. ...the overall increase less dramatic
9	See sample answer in the Treasure Chest

Question Type 5 - Chart

Activity #	Answer
1	a) present simple
2	Possible answer: "increased for all age groups but more rapidly for the middle and older age ranges."
3	b
4	Possible answers: age ranges, (the 75+) category, over 75s, age cohorts, those between (18 and 54), (35-44) year-olds
5	i) a , ii) c , iii) a, iv) b
6	A,D,E
7	See sample answer in the Treasure Chest

Writing Task 2

Question Type 1 - Choose your point of view and support it	
Activity #	**Answer**
1	a
2	c
3	b) or a) if short of time
4	c
5	a
6	c
7	people (consumers); selfish (self-centred); careless (less disciplined)
8	a) Shopping is likely to grow in popularity. b) Shopping is not likely to die out. c) Overspending is likely to cause problems. d) It is highly unlikely that shopping will ever bring happiness.
9	a) Shopping makes consumers selfish. b) Shopping makes consumers dangerous. c) Shopping makes people spend unwisely. d) Shopping makes consumers ill-disciplined.
10	c
11	a) ...enable them to pay their bills b) ...are available to help...
12	c
13	Possible answers: a)...higher education is important b)...travelling has become so popular c)...people work so hard d) Love
14	show (depict); shoppers (consumers); not good enough (inadequate); goods (products); wish (desire); look (appearance); feeling good (wellbeing); social good (community welfare)
15	a, b
16	Possible answers: a) less / more, b) less / more c) more d) more
17	d
18	c
19	b
20	a) + b) – c) + d) –
21	a
22	a) all too / far too all too / far too b) ever-growing c) ever-busier d) never-ending
23	b, c, e
24	See sample answer in the Treasure Chest

Answers

Writing Task 2

Question Type 2 - Present a Two-sided Discussion	
Activity #	**Answer**
1	c
2	b
3	b
4	a
5	b
6	a
7	a) economic uncertainties, b) pure romance is under challenge
8	a) problem, b) issue, c) topic, d) problems/issues
9	b),d),e)
10	a) iii, b) iv, c) ii, d) i
11	your choice, so answers will vary
12	a) often seem, b) often seem, c) often seem to struggle, d) often seems to know
13	your choices, so answers will vary
14	a) wedding cake, b) marriage ceremony, c) marriage partner, d) job opportunity
15	a) 1, b) 4, c) 2, d) 3
16	a), c)
17	a) commitment / infatuation, b) reputation / proximity, c) nutrition / taste
18	your choices so answers will vary
19	a, d, f
20	See sample answer in the Treasure Chest

Question Type 3 - Discuss Advantages & Disadvantages	
Activity #	**Answer**
1	b
2	c
3	a) pros and cons, b) prolonging work past
4	c
5	1) benefits, 2) enables, 3) seems, 4) provides, 5) individuals
6	Disadvantages: c), Supporting example: a)
7	1. On <u>the</u> other hand, 2. <u>a</u> full time job, 3. <u>the</u> workforce
8	a) demanding, b) remaining, c) undertake, d) prevent
9	b
10	See sample answer in the Treasure Chest

Answers

Writing Task 2

Question Type 4 - Discuss Advantages & Disadvantages	
Activity #	**Answer**
1	b
2	c
3	Your choices, so answers will vary.
4	a) tight work schedules, b) the key to making family life better
5	a) First of all / In the first place b) Lastly / Finally c) All in all / Taken together d) So / Consequently e) In the same way / Similarly f) Thereby / thus g) Putting it another way / In other words h) The result of this is / As a result i) Such that / so... that j) This can lead to a situation in which / This can mean that
6	Possible answers: a) Line 1: fundamental change, sufficient change or vital change b) Line 3: most significant social task' c) Line 4: fundamental value / important value / vital value / most significant value d) Line 5: sufficient time / vital time / important time e) Line 5: vital role / important role / fundamental role f) Line 5: empathetic relationships / vital relationships
7	Correct answer: a) harder and longer work, b) less family time
8	Your conclusion, so answer will vary
9	See sample answer in the Treasure Chest

Speaking Activities Answers

Part 1 Q	Answer	Explanation
1	b	a) is too short, and even sounds a little rude c) is still too abrupt and too general
2	c	a) 'place' here means the house, not the suburb b) not sufficiently relevant as it introduces the 'landlord'
3	b	a) too repetitive c) too much hesitation
4	a	b) not polite enough c) asks for an explanation, which assessor can't give
5	b	a) and c) have grammatical problems and lack linking expressions – they are unclear
6		'I have **loads** of friends......some from right back when I was at school, from various jobs I've had, and there are the friends I play **sport** with. I've always been a **friendly** sort of person so I find it easy to **get** on with people when I **meet** them. But, I suppose I'd say I only have one or two **true** friends – friends I completely trust, I **mean**.'
7	a	b) and c) don't have the higher level vocabulary and idioms that a) has (t**o catch up with** my old friends, **bump into** my new friends, **hang out** together).
8	c	
9	b	
10	a	b) and c) use only simpler links: 'and / but / because / so' ; a) uses a wider range: 'even though / however / because / as'
11	c	a) talks more about roads; b) talks about roads and cars (not traffic)
12	b	b) is too direct because it has imperatives, which often seem impolite ('Think about it') and also uses the short, direct forms which can sound abrupt and opinionated ('They can't. It's not possible'). a) and c) use less direct language which sounds more polite.
13	b	Unlike b), responses a) and c) don't show the wider range of strategies for managing hesitation and for retaining a sense of fluency.
14 *	1) I'm sorry, • I didn't catch that. • Could you repeat it, • please?	
	2) Yes • it's great.• There are plenty of parks, • with tennis courts • and many native plants • flowers • and trees.	
	3) As I said just before • I'm a bit shy • but I make friends quite easily • maybe because I'm a good listener • and I like asking questions • and showing interest in people.	
15 *	a) It's **NOR**mal to have a **lot** of **FAM**ily ar**oun**d you.	
	b) ...**so** the in**CREA**sing **lev**els of **TRA**ffic are **very NO**ticeable.	
	c) It's **pro**bably un**LIK**ely that **CAR acc**idents can be s**TO**pped com**PLETE**ly.	
	d) ...I'm a **goo**d **LI**stener and I **like** asking **QUE**stions and **show**ing **IN**terest in **peo**ple.	
16 *	a) I **REALLY LOVE** my family, esp**EC**ially my grandmother; she's such a **BEAUT**iful woman.	
	b) I make friends **REALLY EAS**ily; in fact I get **SUPER** excited when I meet new people.	
	c) I'm a **TERR**ible driver. I get **TO**tally nervous in heavy traffic, and when I get out of the car I feel like a **TO**tal **WRECK**! **SO** I'm annoyed with myself about it!	

Part 2 Q	Answer	Explanation
1	Various	Not Applicable
2 1)	a), d)	Not Applicable
2 2)	e), g)	Not Applicable
2 3)	b), c), h), i), j)	Not Applicable
2 4)	k), f)	Not Applicable
3	b)	(a) is too abrupt and has no introductory sentence; (c) is rather repetitive and suggests the speaker lacks 'true' fluency and flexibility; (b) has a short introduction and establishes some expectation in the listener.
4	a), b)	(a) is unable to use linking words to make his talk smoother and more connected; (b) is uncertain of correct grammar and creates too much hesitation through self-correction.
5	b)	(a) has poor grammar and wanders away from a focused answer by starting to talk about himself rather than his brother; (c) also drifts away from the question by focusing on what his brother did rather than why his brother's life interests him
6	c)	(a) and (b) are very short and direct statements, which often sound a little impolite; in (c) the use of 'I think', and '..for now, anyway' helps to soften the ending and makes it sound more polite by extending it a little;
7	c)	(a) and (b) are too repetitive (lack richness) and thus less interesting

Part 2 Complete Talk

Interviewer: *Could you start now, please?*

Candidate: All right. Well, I suppose all lives are fascinating in some ways, but I'd like to talk briefly about my brother, Pierre. His life has been really extraordinary, at least in my opinion. Let me explain. My brother, Pierre, in fact he's my older brother, as there's five years' difference in our ages, was born in Paris, actually very close to the centre of Paris, where our parents had a very popular, local bakery. Although he was born deaf, Pierre was brilliant at school, especially at mathematics and Art. He also loved the outdoor life and always liked water. As a teenager, I think he was about 14, he went on a course and learned how to sail. He took to sailing like a duck to water, I suppose you could say. After finishing school, he sailed solo to New Zealand in a small sailing boat. This seemed amazing... and really adventurous to me, his little brother, especially as I was a bit of a stay-at-home geek, ...at that time, anyway. Now, where was I? Oh yes. In New Zealand, he met a beautiful, Maori girl, actually she's not deaf, and eventually they got married. He went to Art School over there and is now a well-recognised artist. I've seen some of his work...it's pretty good. He paints landscapes mainly, or to be more precise, I should say, seascapes. I suppose my brother has always seemed especially interesting to me because he was born deaf and as children this created distance between us. As a younger brother I wanted to look up to him, but it was not easy as his disability made him seem so different, so self-contained and unique. But he inspired me because he has many talents, and never let his deafness stop him from taking risks, or from seeking adventure. In some ways, he is still a mystery to me, always intriguing, almost a bit mythical. Er...I think that's all I have to say on this topic, ...for now, anyway.

Interviewer: *Thank you. Do you see your brother very often?*

Candidate: Not as often as I'd like. He came over to Paris last year for our parents' 30th wedding anniversary but flights are a bit too expensive for us to get together regularly.

Answers

Part 3 Q	Answer	Explanation
1	b	(b) is probably the most effective response as it provides two good examples of exciting activities and then develops one of those activities (boar hunting) in an interesting way. (a) offers plenty of examples but they are not really relevant to the idea of 'exciting'. Also, this response loses its focus by starting to talk about money and personal interests. (c) starts well by questioning the meaning of 'excitement' but then just talks about personal things, and loses relevance. NOTE: Responses (a) and (c) might negatively affect final score on 'fluency and coherence' because examiners usually can sense if a candidate is 'filling' time with 'easy to use' language rather than having enough richness, flexibility and control.
2	c	(c) seems the most natural, as the candidate is genuinely reflecting on his/her own reasons and then suggesting that caution is not unusual. The candidate doesn't seem to feel any sense of shame in admitting a sort of lack of courage, which is a personal style of response quite common among adults in western-style cultures. (a) is also an honest response but seems abrupt because it has no 'lead-in' expressions such as 'I like to think that I'm...' in response (c). The examiner might consider this response a little too direct and unsubtle. (b) This response contradicts the questioner, but contradicting in response to a question is fine. However, again, this response is also a little too direct and fails to give any reasons, in response to the 'why' in the question. So it's not really a very relevant answer either.
3	c	c) is the response which has the greatest variety of sentence connecting expressions (because / even though / however / who are...) Although this response sounds a little more formal than the others as a result, it is displaying flexibility of grammar more effectively than the other responses. (a) and (b) sound natural and have good vocabulary but display less variety of clause connection.
4	a	(a) has the richest use of vocabulary (a whole host of reasons, / generally speaking / the pressure of building a career / struggle to find permanent / a succession of temporary positions / feel financially secure / face the responsibility / depend on both partners / potential to earn / is put off) (b) and (c) are good, relevant answers but are a little more repetitive in terms of vocabulary use - the word 'jobs' for example is over-used.
5	b	(b) is the most competent at linking ideas in a varied way (Even though... / more .... than / in terms of... / While... / Compared to... / For example,.. / whereas... / because... /so from that point of view...). (a) and (c) are good answers but rely a little too much on simple linkers such as 'but' or 'and' or 'so' to link ideas.

* **Note:** slight variations are possible.

www.ingramcontent.com/pod-product-compliance
Lightning Source LLC
Chambersburg PA
CBHW051209290426
44109CB00021B/2395